Farley,
Our nation is indebted
others like you who ga
to keep America free - Thank you
for your Service. Fondly,
Effie
September, 2005

Soldiers
Medal

P.F.C.
Parshal H.
Harris
Co "B", 156th Inf

Capt.
Mayhall

CRANKING UP
A FINE WAR

CRANKING UP A FINE WAR

A Louisiana Soldier from Boot Camp to General's Aide

Col. Van R. Mayhall, USAR Ret.

ByrenLee Press · Austin, Texas · Riverdale, New York

Frontispiece: B Company turns out for inspection during a parade in England. Opposite Table of Contents: Lt. Songy and Capt. Mayhall in England.

Unless otherwise credited, photographs are from the author's collection.

Distributed by D+66 Books
7635 Jefferson Hwy., PMB 165
Baton Rouge, LA 70809
dplus66@hieran.com * http://www.hieran.com/dplus66

Printed in the United States of America

Publisher's Cataloging-in-Publication Data
(Prepared by Quality Books, Inc.)

Mayhall, Van R., 1919–
     Cranking up a fine war : a Louisiana soldier
from boot camp to general's aide / Van R. Mayhall.
— 1st ed.
     p.   cm.
LCCN: 98-89821
ISBN: 1-892958-01-5

     1. Mayhall, Van R., 1919– 2. World War,
1939–1945—Personal narratives, American.
3. United States.—Army—Officers—Biography.
I. Title.

D811.M39   1999   940.54'81'73
                                        QBI98-1759

10   9   8   7   6   5   4   3   2   1

To my one love,
Marie

Table of Contents

Foreword

When I first began to write this account, I called it *D+66* for the day I landed at Normandy—two months after D-Day, the date from which we started counting the drive toward the end of the war in Europe. But this book begins long before D-Day and continues past D-plus-66-days, across the Atlantic, England, and France and into Germany.

My granddaughter, Robin Mayhall, nudged me into sorting out some of the stories that had happened to me as I grew up, joined the military, and went to Europe. So I looked at my footlocker full of V-Mail—ribbon-tied stacks of letters to my wife, Marie Roques Mayhall, that I had written before and after we were married; and I looked at the poorly kept diary that I wrote in now and then while I was overseas. I thought if I could put down some of the stories as I remembered them, the V-Mail and diary would help sort the details and dates. I hoped that this would be written well enough so that some of the grandchildren—my own and those of other veterans—would read it and pass the story along to the generations after them.

Van R. Mayhall, Colonel USAR Ret.
Baton Rouge, Louisiana

Introduction

Ever since I can remember, my grandfather has been telling war stories. When I was a little girl, sitting with my cousins around the fireplace at my grandparents' house, they were just that—stories—tales of places I could only vaguely imagine and of events that seemed very far removed from me.

I listened to the stories then because I loved my Grand-D and he liked talking about "the War." It wasn't until I matured myself that I began to see his stories as much more than just tales. They are truly a part of history, a living history woven into the fabric of all that makes our nation special.

When I was in college, Grand-D sent me a few stories he had written. They were suddenly much more interesting and informative than I had remembered. Beyond that, I realized they were well written—that my grandfather has a gift for capturing people and events in a very genuine and often humorous way. Wanting to preserve the stories for my family, I transcribed them from the manuscript, laboriously handwritten on a series of yellow legal pads, to my computer.

I never thought publishing Grand-D's stories as a book was anything more than a pleasant wish until I met my dear friend Carol Burrell, whose publishing knowledge was outstripped only by her enthusiasm for the project. She gave me the impetus to push the project forward, and together we encouraged my grandfather to turn his stories into a narrative. What you are holding now is the product of more than ten years of hard work on the part of Grand-D, his editor, and me.

I hope you will enjoy this book as much as I have. I'm glad to have been part of the project. Most of all, I'm proud of my grandfather. Not only because he has produced a genuinely interesting and valuable memoir, but because of the very events of the story itself. My grandfather fought in the Battle of the Bulge; he landed at Normandy on D-plus-66 and helped liberate France. I thank him for his perseverance in writing this memoir, and I thank him for serving our country.

Last but not least, I love him for being my Grand-D.

Robin M. Mayhall
Austin, Texas

CRANKING UP
A FINE WAR

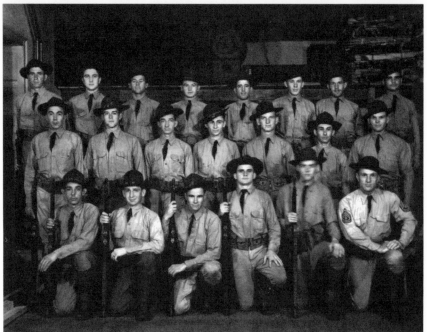

National Guard

*I*n 1936 I started wearing uniforms of one kind or another. I had a little discussion with my mother about the National Guard. My older brother Carney Allen, C.A., had been in the Guard before he departed Baton Rouge to go to work for Shell Oil. Seventeen years old was not old enough for me to sign up on my own, so Mother and Dad had to give me permission to follow in C.A.'s footsteps. I felt like I should join the Guard and get some experience in uniform. The Germans were cranking up a fine war in Europe, and it looked like it would last long enough for me to want to know something about how to fight. This point I stressed with Mother, so Mother agreed to sign my papers.

Besides getting a nice uniform, I got to march around with a beautiful rifle, model 1903, bolt action, clip fed. I could feel the reassuring weight of the bayonet slapping my hip as I walked along and the counterweight of the canteen hanging over my left rear pocket. With the campaign hat, I felt that I looked like one of our country's finest. Not only that, they were paying me a dollar for every drill I made, four dollars every month, paid out every three months. We also got to go to camp each year for two weeks—fourteen dollars for all that happy living, running around in the boondocks.

When we went off to summer camp everything came alive. Our company joined up with other companies and became a battalion, and the battalions joined with the other battalions to form the Regiment. Then the whole Regiment would come together on the parade ground at the end of camp for Regimental Review. This was very impressive to a young soldier: the band playing the old marches, the orders coming down to form the parade to pass in review.

On the way to that Regimental Review, we were out on the rifle range, machine-gun range, mortar range, hand-grenade range, and the bayonet range, learning the beginnings of what a soldier is supposed to know.

I was still in Catholic High School and would finish in the spring of 1937. I was very carried away with boxing and football, and I had high hopes that some small college would let me play more football. I had gained weight and height; I was up to 155 pounds and about five-foot-nine. My father said, "If you want to go to Louisiana State, I'll pay half and you pay half." I had to find a job.

Bennie Ruhl, for whom I had worked as lifeguard at City Park, asked me to go to Alexandria, Louisiana, with him as his head lifeguard to open up a new pool and train people to run it. I didn't have to think about this very long. I was a qualified Senior Red Cross Life Saver and Red Cross Instructor, so off we went. At the end of the summer I had saved enough to go to LSU but by then Bennie was trying to talk me into going to the Royal Canadian Air Force instead, to get into the action overseas. This was something else I would have needed my parents to sign for.

Mother thought I had lost my mind, so I went to LSU. Bennie went into the RCAF.

■　■　■

In spite of boxing, football, fishing, hunting, and lifeguarding, I had met Marie. She was the dream girl I had always hoped to meet some day. Marie and I walked down the same street to go back and forth to school. We started studying together—this may have improved our writing a little bit because we sat at her Mama's dining room table to work and couldn't talk, so we had to pass notes to each other. We played tennis, went swimming, took in school functions, and went to more dances than I can remember.

One of our first trips together was to New Orleans—with permission from our parents. I dressed in my best clothes and walked to Marie's house. We walked to the station at the bottom

Above: Lifeguards at City Park, Alexandria, Louisiana. Summer 1936.

of the hill in front of the old state capitol and got on the train. The train pulled into New Orleans, and we began walking again. We got to the French Quarter and visited Arnaud's and Antoine's and SeLario's and saw all the different kinds of food those New Orleans people ate.

New Orleans food was a great curiosity to me. In Baton Rouge the little stores didn't have great variety. SeLario's had a dozen kinds of cheeses, mysterious fruit of all kinds, salami from overseas made of donkey meat, blood sausage, and long strings of wieners hung from racks. Dried beans in hundred pound sacks sat on the floor, open at the top; I only recognized the black-eyed peas. In the middle of all this produce, there were men ready to make you the most delicious sandwiches with any garnish you could think of on New Orleans French bread. Arnaud's, Antoine's, Galatoire's, and other fine restaurants served trout, turtle soup, Oysters Rockefeller, and Shrimp Creole, just to start.

How we got back to the train I will never know. I had never been in New Orleans before. I didn't know where the street cars went. We certainly didn't have money for taxis. We did a lot of walking and did a lot of asking.

Above, left: Van Mayhall on the Catholic High football team; right: Marie Roques in 1937. Below, left: Van and Marie on a trip to New Orleans; right: Pvt. Mayhall, serving as general's aide for a day.

The trip to New Orleans must have been some kind of magic because I loved Marie from then on. I never dated anyone else.

We had a standing date on Sunday nights. Sometimes we sat on the steps or front porch or we walked. Money was always scarce. Some Saturdays we would go to the dances at the American Legion Hall; after the dance if we had enough to buy a cherry coke we would walk to Walgreens.

Fall 1937 I turned up as a freshman at LSU. This is when I began to notice that I would have been better off if I had enjoyed studying as much as I did football and boxing and dances. I quickly found other interests. Here was a new type of uniform, that of a Reserve Officer Training Corps Cadet. I did not know at the time that if I signed up for Chemical Engineering I would be put in the Artillery Battalion of the Cadet Corps. So here I was in the Infantry National Guard and the Artillery at LSU. The two didn't interfere with each other, and I liked them both. I soon recognized that my problem was the Chemical Engineering. I was having a wonderful time with all the new stuff in which I was involved, but my "head bone" was not word perfect.

School demanded a lot of attention. I went to LSU for three years. Marie went for a year, then to business college, and then went to work here and there. By the time 1940 rolled around, Marie started work at Harding Field military air base, and I was leaving to enlist for a year. I thought about the idea of getting married, but knew I didn't have the financial security.

A three-striped sergeant earned sixty dollars a month. So I made big plans to save all of my pay and propose when the year was over. We wrote each other regularly, and it was always so great to hear "Mayhall" at mail call because I knew that I had a letter from my love. As attractive as Marie was, and with the war scare picking up, more young, handsome men began to show up in town and show interest in her. There was never any agreement between Marie and me, so we were both allowed to date whomever, whenever we wanted. With this freedom it wasn't too long before Marie and I went our separate ways. When it finally dawned on me that I was losing, I stopped writing because I was sure that I was wasting my time.

■　■　■

Camp Blanding 1941

Learning to Live Without Mama

*T*he artillery batteries at LSU took part in all the cadet corps competitions, so we were quickly involved in uniform competition (shined brass, shined shoes, pressed uniforms), marching, parading. Once a week there was a cadet corps parade on the parade ground in front of the Memorial Tower. Then there was the athletic competition: the cross-country relay, the boxing intramurals, and the swimming. All these activities were in the name of getting a point for the battery. I was in the extra radio classes. I was in the extra drill platoon, and the demonstration firing battery.

I liked every bit of the military, and I was fairly sure the military liked me. However, at the end of my second year at LSU I was not appointed to Advanced Military. I had paid too little attention to the academic part of my first two years, so my grades were not good enough. With nothing else to do, I began to learn a little bit more about what I was supposed to have been learning before. Trying to bring up my grades, I went to the shops and took all they had: woodworking, welding, and auto mechanics.

My grades did come up, but other things were happening. The President had ordered the National Guard on active duty for a year to train. The National Guard had promoted me to a Platoon Sergeant.

I was ready to go, all the way to training camp in Florida. I had never been away from home to amount to anything, so this was real excitement. Marie and her parents came down to the station where we were loading on the train to leave. This, of course, made me feel more important than ever. This departure happened on December 22, 1940. We arrived in a place I had never heard of called Camp Blanding, close to a small town named Starke. We arrived in one of the coldest winters that northern Florida had had in many years.

We were supposed to have winterized tents, but most of them were just plain tents. The company street was ankle deep in mud. We discovered that we could get things done a whole lot faster if we did them ourselves. The first thing we did was to borrow enough lumber to winterize our tents. Then we borrowed enough lumber to make "duck walks" up and down the streets. Someone had put a large pile of sawdust in the battalion area that was supposed to be used for something. We got a night detail out and borrowed all of that sawdust and spread it in the company street. After we had enough of it, it made solid footing so that we didn't get muddy-wet every time we had to assemble.

We had about half of the company in the hospital in the first month and a half. We were not used to living under the conditions of rain, cold, and wet. Flu spread through the company in a hurry. Conditions gradually improved: hot water for showers, small wood-burning heaters for the winterized tents. The kitchen crews learned to use the equipment, which meant better meals. We learned to take better care of ourselves.

Learning to live away from home: Mama wasn't there any more. Many of our people were not twenty years old. We had some as young as sixteen. We marched, we drilled, we crawled, we ran, we jumped, we washed our mess utensils and our underclothes. We shined shoes and buttons, cleaned rifles, teamed up for company baseball and softball. We soon found that in addition to being proficient in marching, shooting, knife-fighting, and drilling with machine guns, pistols, and bayonets, the Division Commander wanted his whole division to be able to march twenty miles a day.

When a division marches twenty miles a day, there is an I.P., initial point, and twenty miles down the road there is an R.P., release point. A division has about twenty thousand men in it, so you can see that it would be difficult for them all to be sitting

Above: Would-be lieutenants "Wolf" Riser and Van Mayhall.

on the I.P. when someone shouts "Forward!" Every unit comes from its assigned bivouac area; the bivouac is an area to which a division, regiment, battalion, company or platoon is assigned to pitch tents, set up kitchens, set up water supply, dig latrines, and generally make as comfortable as possible for the length of time the units will be there. At the end of that time, the kitchen is closed, the tents are struck, the latrines are covered, and the units are supposed to make it look as if no one had ever been there.

When the bivouac is closed, the units start out. Each unit has a time at which it is to cross the I.P. If the 1st Company of the 1st Battalion of the 1st Regiment has operation orders to cross the I.P. at 0700, that is where that 1st Company had better be. Now, there is a little problem when a regiment is in bivouac. The units are scattered all over the place. That 1st Company might be five miles from the I.P., so the company has to start early enough to cover those five miles. Of course, everyone is surprised if they successfully cross. The General Division C.O. and the Regimental C.O. stand there, checking their watches, doubting anyone will get there on time.

I had been assigned to A½ Company, which was the training company for the newly arriving "selectees." We were to bring these people up to speed with the rest of the company. I felt so bad about what had happened between Marie and me—no longer writing each other—and was so distracted that I was sent back to my regular company. This shook me out of my gloom, and I went back to work to see what I could make of myself while in the Army. I trained hard, studied hard, and qualified myself with all of the weapons I could get my hands on.

I was becoming a better soldier, a better sergeant. The Company Commander called in Sergeant Henry "Wolf" Riser and myself one day and told us that the Army would need officers soon and that we should start studying—the test would be given later on in the spring. Wolf Riser and I did finally get around to studying the last two weeks before the test. We studied all night every other night. We would leave the mess hall

Below: At Camp Blanding, on a duck walk. Right: The Company Commander was so confident Van Mayhall had passed the test for promotion to 2nd Lieutenant, he issued officer's web equipment early.

where we had permission to study, put on field uniforms, and drill all day. The day came, and the test seemed rather easy. It never occurred to us that it was difficult until we found out that the 1st Sergeant of D Company had failed. We were really surprised.

Our papers were sent off to the Infantry School at Fort Benning, Georgia, for processing, and it seemed that they would never get back. It took so long that we just forgot about them.

I went on with my duties as Platoon Sergeant and was taking everything one day at a time. We were camping out in the field doing squad and platoon tactics, and for entertainment digging turtles out of the ground and chasing squirrels.

On a day in June the 1st Sergeant called me in and asked me if I wanted to go home on furlough. We had been in for six months, so I was due ten days. I didn't really think I had any good reason to go home right then, and there was a 120-mile march that the whole division was taking part in at the end of June. I told the 1st Sergeant that I wanted to make the march with my platoon and that I would go home later.

Well, I didn't get to go home in 1941 at all. We began our march in Ocala National Forest, and it was late. A runner came down from Battalion hollering, "Sgt. Mayhall, Sgt. Mayhall, hurry up and come to Battalion and sign your papers so you'll be paid for today as a 2nd Lieutenant." The next day the Captain sent me into camp to buy some uniforms fitting my new rank. My time started over on June 30, 1941, so I wouldn't have leave to go home until Christmas.

■ ■ ■

The Louisiana Maneuvers

*T*hat whole year, 1941, was busy. There was much activity, travel, training, maneuvers, study, and growing. The first months we trained in all of the individual talents that a soldier has to learn in order to maintain himself. Then we went into squad tactics, platoon tactics, and company tactics. We stomped down scrub oak and palmetto all over the Camp Blanding training ground. We marched, we walked, we crouched, we crawled, we slid across the fields, the woods, the mud puddles, crossed the streams in daytime, nighttime, and in the rain. All of this was in the name of becoming confident in one's own self, so that we would be able to outmaneuver our opponents, able to kill without being killed.

Midsummer 1941, orders came down for a big move. The 31st Division would take part in Louisiana maneuvers in Kisatchie Natural Forest for three months. We had trained so hard that we felt we could hold up our end.

Going through Baton Rouge would be a big thing for A Company. Some of us hadn't been home at all yet. Our last bivouac before passing through Baton Rouge was at one of the parks at Mandeville, Louisiana. The people who knew passed the word in Baton Rouge that we would not be able to stop there. Much to our surprise when we arrived in Mandeville there was a busload of mothers, wives, and children who had come to see their soldier boys. My mother came with other mothers on the school bus.

I was still on special detail following the division, so I got in late, but the reunion with home folks—the presents, homemade cookies, and candy—was just great.

The next day the division was on the road again, and as we entered Baton Rouge I wondered if Marie knew I was passing through. I guessed I knew then that for me, whatever we had between us wasn't quite over.

Our next bivouac was a little place I had never heard of called Sugar Town. This put us in position for the beginning of the Louisiana maneuvers. The second night we were there, all bedded down in our pup tents, a rainstorm showed up. Having lived in a house and camp for so long, I had never experienced a real Louisiana rainstorm in the open. The area we were in was nice and flat so that rain flooded everything; about everybody and everything got wet. Blankets, clothing, rifles, webbing had to be dried. As soon as this little problem was over with, we were on the move.

We seemed to be moving north from Sugar Town. The next night we didn't get bed rolls or shelter halls. We just found a place and bedded down. We were under low-hanging trees and found some rather comfortable depressions in the ground. We found out the next day that we were enjoying some sheep wallows. Thank goodness the sheep had taken most of their fleas with them (but not all of them).

We moved into position to surprise an opposing unit. The area was covered with tall dry grass and we were well hidden. We found that not all of our commanding officers were that much at home in the field. We were lying very quiet when we heard someone kicking the grass as he walked toward my platoon.

It was Lt. Col. Wright, the C.O. of 1st Battalion, 156th Infantry. He seemed to be lost, and he began to call for his adjutant, 1st Lt. J. Hillary Boh.

"Boh.

"Boh?

"Hey, Boh!"

The closer to my platoon he got, the greater his panic. He finally got into the middle of my platoon still hollering for Boh.

I couldn't let him walk out past my platoon because there was no one in front of us. I stood up and called to the Colonel. He jumped like I had shot at him. I asked him if he needed a little help, and he told me he was looking for the 1st Battalion. I told him he was in it.

Above: Scenes from the Louisiana Maneuvers.

Opposite: Scenes from the Louisiana Maneuvers. Above: Bedding down for the night in a graveyard.

He wanted to know where they were, and I told him again he was in the middle of 1st Platoon, A Company.

He told me he couldn't see any of them and wanted them to stand up.

I had my platoon stand up and show themselves. He was surrounded. He looked at them, looked at me, and took off in the direction he had come from. I don't think I saw him again the rest of the time we spent in Louisiana. I am sure he didn't go far without Boh.

We moved from one area to another in blocking positions and flanking positions. We must have been very elusive. I never quite understood General Patton's remarks about the Louisiana maneuvers. Patton was control officer for the maneuvers, testing the new mechanization of the army. His report made comments about what a poor job we had done. We never saw him or any of his troops or any of his horses, but we must have kept his troops on the run. We travelled one hundred fifty-six miles in three and a half days. I walked the heels off two pairs of shoes.

When we finally stopped we were fourteen miles outside of Shreveport. It was beginning to frost a little by that time. Most of the time we didn't get to undress. There was no point, since we didn't have any other clothes to put on. We slept in what we had on. One night I slept on half of my raincoat and covered with the other half. When I picked up my raincoat the next morning, a copperhead went sliding away. This little deadly snake had crawled under me for warmth. Had I known that copperhead was there, we would have parted company sooner.

After another full day's march we came across a graveyard. It was in good condition, cleaned out and the grass trimmed. It was just a country graveyard—we were not close to any towns or houses. The company had walked twenty-five miles that day, and no one noticed any ghosts slipping around, so we slept right there. I slept between two senior ladies. They didn't seem to mind and neither did I.

■   ■   ■

There can't be that many people running around in the woods, mingled with tanks, trucks, and horse cavalry, without someone getting hurt.

While one man was sleeping a truck backed over his head. Fortunately, the soil was sandy and the truck pushed his head into the sand, and nothing happened that an aspirin wouldn't cure. I would think that there was a certain amount of panic when this soldier woke up with a truck wheel on his head, to say nothing of the fact he would probably be more careful about choosing a sleeping area.

One of the worst accidents and bad decisions that I saw firsthand was along a bayou close to a large sawmill. A Company was on the right flank of the regiment and there was a company from West Virginia on our right. This was the only time I saw the enemy on this maneuver. They had been firing blanks as we moved up. We had been shouting the normal insults at the West Virginia outfit. We had orders to move up to the bayou and stop and wait for more orders. The West Virginia outfit decided they would cross the bayou.

They hung their rifles around their necks and they rushed in. Some dove head first. It had been so hot, it looked like a good way to cool off. No one checked the depth of this bayou at this place, and with the packs on their backs and rifles around their necks it was the beginning of a mass drowning three yards from the bank.

The sawmill had a pipe sticking down into the bayou. This was where water was pumped to cool whatever needed cooling. Years of pumping water from this area had made the bayou very deep.

I suppose the West Virginia troops thought they would just walk across the bayou. All of these soldiers were headed for the bottom with the weight they had strapped to their backs. A whole platoon went underwater.

The people behind them immediately started trying to get them out. I told my Company Commander I had been a lifeguard and got permission to try to find the last few. We found some in deep water; trying to get their packs off of their backs they had gotten their arms pinned to their sides and had given up. Fortunately, there were a number of other people who knew lifesaving techniques and pumped water out of them.

I never found out how many soldiers died that day, but it sure was a lousy move.

■ ■ ■

The plan of maneuver must have been for the 156th Infantry to move to a blocking position, because the opposing troops were withdrawing toward Shreveport. The whole regiment was on the march from daylight until after dark.

A Company from Baton Rouge felt a whole lot more confident about ourselves. We had done everything required of us on this three-month maneuver. Every man who started was still with us when the maneuver was over. When time came for us to leave for Camp Blanding, our home camp, the word came down that the Commanding General was pleased, so furloughs and leaves could be given. I still didn't have enough leave time to go home, so I went back to Camp Blanding.

■ ■ ■

Off We Went

The word had been put out that we were being sent to North Carolina for a month for winter maneuvers. It must have been late October when we started. The move from Blanding to North Carolina was supposed to be tactical, a move under combat conditions. My assignment was flank protection. I was given three half-ton trucks, four men to each vehicle. Our job was to cover the right flank of the regiment as we made the move. We were supposed to run the roads to be sure the enemy were not lying in wait for our main column.

We had lots of fun tearing around the country roads, easing up to hills before we were exposed, and looking over the tops to be sure we weren't spotted and fired on. We would dash from one place to another; when I say dash, I do mean dash. I believe I managed to get three of the wildest drivers in the battalion. Skidding around curves, throwing gravel all over the place. The country roads were not blacktopped. We did have a little trouble keeping up with the main column. The main column would turn without putting the information out to us riding the flanks. There were some times when we were eating sardines and crackers at little bitty country stores wondering where the main column went.

The weather was beginning to turn cold and rainy, and we seemed to always get into the bivouac after chow time. On one particular night we came in after dark, and it was raining. The half-ton trucks went back to their units to be gassed up and checked over for the next day. We had managed to find something to eat, and I had to report in to whomever. After that, I

21

went looking for a place to bed down. No pup tents were pitched; my bed roll was somewhere other than where I was. Some headquarters tents were pitched. I wandered around looking in these tents; men were sleeping on the ground in them. I looked in trucks, under trucks, for a place to get out of the rain and get some sleep.

Here I was, an important 2nd Lieutenant with four months seniority, with no shelter! I finally worked up a plan. I found a spot on the side of a slight hill among some pine trees where no trucks could run over my head, wrapped my raincoat around me a little tighter, lay down, pulled my feet up as far as I could, turned up my collar, put my helmet over my upturned ear, and went to sleep. I am sure my mother would have thought we would catch all sorts of colds, flu, and pneumonia, but we must have been sleeping outdoors long enough that some natural resistance had taken over. I felt no ill effects from this sort of experience. When all else fails, to hell with it.

We reached Charleston, South Carolina, on a miserable freezing night. It was so cold that the commanding officers thought some of us troops might freeze to death. So we marched up and down the streets of the town until daylight to keep from freezing. Finally we moved into the area where we were to set up camp. It was in a National Forest with a lot of young trees. Orders came down that we were to help out a forest ration project by cutting the low branches off, up to head high. This would have been fine for starting fires, but we were not allowed to cut any trees big enough to make a real fire.

We did some reconnaissance work, trying to look over the area we would be moving around in. One day the sun came out and it warmed up. Some of us started thinking it would be nice to find a place to bathe. Someone announced that there was a creek not far away, so with soap and towel off we went. We got to a clear rocky waterway. We quickly stripped down to our birthday suits and everything was fine until I stepped into that creek water up to my ankles and turned blue to my knees. I quickly determined that I didn't need a bath near as bad as I thought. I exploded from the cold, cold creek, quickly climbed back into my clothes. That creek water had made chickens out of the whole group. The last remark I heard leaving our wonderful bathing place was, "Well, everybody still smells the same."

I often wondered what the visit to North Carolina was supposed to teach us about, and the only thing that I could come up with was weather. I was never oriented on what the maneuver was or whom we were maneuvering against. We found out what it felt like to sleep on the ground in pup tents and with no pup tents, in rain, sleet, and snow. It taught every soldier to remember where he last left his overcoat, raincoat, dry socks, long underwear, gloves, scarf, and anything else that he could put on to stay warm. The loss of one glove could make a soldier no use on the open field.

This month of winter maneuvers was finally over and we (the 31st Division) went back to Florida. It was getting into late November 1941—which was getting close to December 22. December 22 would end the one year we had enlisted for. There was no war yet. We would all go home. We worked to bring our camp back up to the good condition it was in before we had gone to Louisiana and North Carolina.

Sunday afternoon, about 2:00 P.M. on December 7, I was sitting in my tent writing home to mother. My little radio was on my little shelf. My new copy of *Esquire* was lying on my cot, and I was sipping a little bit of Canadian Club.

My first line was,

> *Dear Mother, I think I will be able to come home*
> *for Christmas.*

The little radio shook me into alertness. It said, "Flash— Pearl Harbor is being bombed by the Japanese." My next line was,

> *Mom, I just heard something on the radio that*
> *makes me think I won't be home for Christmas.*

Well, sure enough I didn't get home for Christmas.

Above: Soldiers training with rifles. (FDR Library)

Immediately, the whole of Camp Blanding was buzzing around like a hive of bees. Orders came down: "Get your regiments ready, get your battalions ready, get your companies ready, get your platoons ready, the division will move. The division will be broken down into battalion combat teams and you will be stationed along the East Coast." East Coast defense! "1st Battalion, 156th Infantry will be the northernmost combat team to be stationed out from Wilmington, North Carolina." That was me, Platoon Leader, A Company, 1st Battalion, 156th Infantry.

As we were climbing into trucks to move, a man who was a freshman with me at LSU but whose name I never knew, went into a boiler room and blew his brains out. He couldn't accept the idea that we were going to war and he was in it up to his neck. This was the first that some of us noticed that this was serious stuff. Within forty-eight hours we were on the road heading north and east.

The 1st Battalion combat team, after riding all day, all night, and most of another day, went through Wilmington, North Carolina, out onto a little place called Fort Fisher. Fort

Above: Sixteen-inch howitzer in place for East Coast defense. (FDR Library)

Fisher was where we unloaded (or detrucked, as the Army says) and began to set up camp. We quickly began to set up defensive positions around Fort Fisher. We set up platoon positions, company positions, battery positions. When we were in position we were all looking out to sea, on alert. Alert! Alerts were called regularly and we would all go dashing and running to our dug-in positions.

In these defensive positions every gun has a specific job to do in what we call final protective fire. In final protective fire, every rifleman has a specific field of fire, every machine gun is pointed so that the fire crosses in front of the position. The mortars are aimed, or "laid," so that the mortar bursts drop into the dips and rolls in the landscape that can't be covered by machine gun and rifle fire.

Part of my work on East Coast defenses was working with
S-2 (Intelligence). We would run up and down talking to the
fishermen living along the coast, checking if any strange boats
had visited the area. There had been some radar sightings of
boats going out and meeting a boat coming in (we suspected a
submarine) and staying together long enough for oil and food to
be transferred. We never got anything except stories that we
could excite each other with and that kept everybody running
when "Alert!" was sounded.

It was cold out there next to the ocean. It snowed, and the
cold winds that blew in from the Atlantic Ocean were numbing.
But with working schedules that kept us busy, the cold wasn't
noticed too much. War had been declared against Japan and
Germany, and we all knew that none of us would be out of the
service until the war was over. None of us had ever considered
that we would have to fight anybody but the Germans. Now the
prospect of going to the Japanese battle zone was something
else to think about and train for. It was around this time when
we began to learn more kinds of fighting. Each form of attack
that an individual could learn made him a more confident soldier and helped him get over the fear of combat. Wrestling, kicking—any and every means of killing was practiced.

By the time Christmas came around, the excitement of war
had cooled down to the point where leaves were being given
out. I was going home for New Year's. I had mixed feelings
about going home. I wanted to see my family, but Marie and I
had been on the outs for six months, and I really didn't know
how I would, could bridge that gap. I did have something going
for me: I was much more self confident. I had grown and
learned a lot, and I no longer wore Sergeant stripes. I had been
commissioned a 2nd Lieutenant. I seemed to stand straighter
and taller.

I arrived home. I don't remember how—train, bus, or automobile. Air travel was not an everyday affair. Mother and Dad
received me with great pride. I could see it in their eyes. Mother
couldn't do enough for me, and Dad took me down to the train
station and introduced me to his friends of many years on the
railroad.

Marie's father, Emile Roques, phoned me after I had been home a couple of days and invited me to supper. I had learned to love the food that "Mama" and "Papa" Roques cooked, so there was no way I would refuse. In addition, I had learned to like and respect Mama and Papa. When the appointed evening arrived, I put on my best front—shined shoes, 2nd Lieutenant bars shined, belt buckle shined, freshly laundered uniform, and off I went. The subject never came up as to whether Papa had needed any urging to call me and make the invitation. I was happy enough about the situation. I would see Marie.

When I came face to face with Marie, the six months of doubt died. I felt my heart skip a beat and I knew I loved her as much as ever. She had had no idea that I was coming home. She had no reason to be interested in my coming home and she had new boyfriends with planned dates for the New Year. However, we made good time with what we had. We made no agreements nor tried to put any limitation on each other. Marie went on with her life and I went on with mine. However, we did begin to write again, and it seemed that the letters had more meaning. In the year that we hadn't seen each other, both of us had grown and matured considerably from where we were when I left Baton Rouge in December 1940. By the time I got on a bus to go back to Fort Fisher, I knew that I had deep feelings—love is a better word—but with what I had facing me in the near future, I had no idea whether we would ever marry.

■ ■ ■

Fresh Orders

I left Baton Rouge and rode for twenty-four hours to get back to Wilmington, North Carolina. The uncomfortable bus trip was worse than the march through the bayou. I slept a good bit of the way, but the people in the next seat pushed me back up straight when I'd used their shoulders for too long.

I arrived in Wilmington after midnight, and it was snowing. It was the day that I was supposed to report for duty. I had coffee and something to eat and then I wondered how I could get out to Fort Fisher twenty miles down the beach. Fortunately, an army truck had been in town to pick up early morning supplies, and I managed to flag him down for the return trip.

I got there and reported to my new Commanding Officer. He said to report to my platoon in the field, but I was in dress uniform. My trunk was still in the bus depot in Wilmington. I had no field clothes. I had had orders to go to Camp Bullis, Texas, when I returned from leave, so I had packed everything that belonged to me, but my orders had been cancelled while I was away. My field clothes were in my trunk.

Wolf Riser told me to take his car and go pick up my trunk. When I got back, dressed in my field clothes, my Commanding Officer was waiting for me. He accused me of disobeying direct orders, which I had done, and he threatened to court-martial me. I tried to explain to him what the circumstances were, but he would have none of my explanation.

I didn't like the situation. As a matter of fact, I was mad as a wet hornet, and I took off for headquarters and went in to see

29

the Battalion Combat Team Commanding Officer. I explained to him what had happened. When I finished the Colonel told me to go about my business and forget it. He said he would take care of it, and he apparently did, because that was the last I ever heard of it.

I went back to doing whatever I had been doing. Along about this time a number of the qualified people in the company made application for Officer Candidate School. I always said to myself and to anybody who would listen that A Company was a good company. Seventeen men from A Company became officers and they did a good job.

One was killed storming the beaches in France. One was killed in Italy at Salerno. One was wounded on the beaches of France, one was wounded in the hedgerows in France, another was wounded in the Hurtgen Forest in Germany. How many more were killed or wounded I don't know. All of them that I knew of had been in "harm's way."

■ ■ ■

Below: A group of friends from A Company. All of them ended up in "harm's way." Crocket (left) became a paratrooper; his plane was mistakenly shot down by Allied fire on his first run over Italy.

I should have expected it, but I didn't. All of a sudden, fresh orders came down. Get ready to move! So we packed everything that belonged to A Company. Kitchen stoves, tents, any and everything went on trucks. After all the equipment, next all the men were assigned to trucks. When we were loaded, the orders came. "Wind them up." "Move out."

We turned south at Wilmington, and I felt fine with the idea of getting out of that cold. The word came down that we were going "home," that is, back to Camp Blanding. We didn't seem to be in as much hurry to get back to Camp Blanding as we were to get to Fort Fisher for the protection of the East Coast. Not seeing anything that looked bad, sounded bad, we all became a little more quiet, settled down, laid back, relaxed, and thoughtful.

The thoughtful business came with the prospect of being in a war no one had any idea how long would last. I had been welding for Delta Tank, making butane storage tanks and mine parts for the Navy, when I went into the service, and I had already decided that welding was not what I wanted to do when I got out. I made up my mind to do the very best that I could while in the service. I had been commissioned; the prospect of going up looked good, for the Army was swelling and in need of leadership. So I worked, studied, and went to what schools I could get.

These same thoughts went through the heads of many of the other people in the company. Some went to the paratroopers, some to the Air Corps, and others looked for slots where they could learn and be promoted also. Supply, transportation, radio, and maintenance all needed good people. I still had no idea all the different kinds of people it took to run a war until I went overseas and saw the thousands of tons of food and equipment, thousands of tanks, thousands of trucks, thousands of cannons, thousands of airplanes, as well as thousands of soldiers, medical supplies, and hospitals. It takes seven men or women working behind the lines to put one fighting man on the front.

■ ■ ■

We arrived in Camp Blanding. It seemed like spring after going through most of December and part of January at Fort Fisher.

We had hardly detrucked when the inspections started: field inspections, equipment inspections, vehicle inspections, and personal inspections. All these were necessary to bring us back to the sharpness of a first-class infantry company. As soon as we had cleaned, shined, marched, and sweated through physical training, we went back to the field for squad, platoon, and company tactics.

For lack of money and places to go, on weekends a few of us would go back into the woods and swamps to see what we could see. During these explorations, we had seen alligators, wild hog tracks, bear tracks, wildcat tracks, deer tracks—to say nothing of the squirrels and rabbits. So we were not always sure what we would find when we were out. On the night of the company exercise, I was ordered to take my platoon to the far side of a long narrow swamp, put the platoon in a blocking position, and report back when they were in place. We started out and went into the swamp; it was so thick and so dark that we came out about the same place we went in. We looked at our overlay map and located a firebreak not too far away, so off we went, found the firebreak, crossed the swamp, and went into the blocking position.

I told my platoon sergeant that I had to report where we were to Company Headquarters. My runner asked if I wanted him to come with me. It was only about one mile back to Headquarters, so I told him to bed down, get a little rest, because nothing would be happening until daylight. Off I went.

It had turned cloudy. I found the firebreak and started through. It was so dark I couldn't see the trees and bushes on either side. I felt my way along and got to the middle of the firebreak. All of a sudden some good-sized animal broke cover, went across the firebreak from left to right, and stopped. It startled me so bad that I jumped straight up in the air and had my .45 pistol out of my buckled holster before my feet hit the ground. Of course, the pistol was empty. We were not allowed to carry ammunition at the time. There I was trying to see something in the dark; whatever was facing me was doing the same.

Whatever it was, it was breathing very hard, loud enough to be a bear.

The breathing seemed to quiet down a little bit. It never occurred to me to turn back to the platoon—I had to report. I started making small, curious steps to get by "whatever" and the farther past "it" I got, the faster I got. By the time I got to the edge of the swamp I was in full gallop and trying for even greater speed. Fortunately, I had ample time between the swamp and Company Headquarters to regain composure. I would have hated to run through Headquarters like a tiger—or a bear—was on my tail. Glad I didn't have any bullets for my .45. I might have been the only one in the regiment who had a War.

I had some thoughts about going back through the swamp. However, I was saved from this by the Company Commander, who said, "Mayhall, you'd better stay at Headquarters tonight and go back to your platoon at daylight." It was the relief that comes when the dentist says, "No cavities." This was the last field trip at Camp Blanding; shortly, we received new orders.

The division was to exchange camps with the 36th Infantry, Texas National Guard. We thought for a moment we would be closer to Baton Rouge, but after looking at the maps a little bit knew better. We already knew we were six hundred miles to the east of Baton Rouge. After the move we would be about seven hundred miles to the west. Moving was always excitement. Change was good for us, so we got loaded up and were ready to move.

■ ■ ■

Bivouac in the Blue Norther

I don't know how I managed to get another detail that would make my travelling easier, but I did. I was assigned to follow the regiment with three half-ton trucks and check all of the bivouac areas to be sure that everything was in the same order that it was before the regiment arrived. Signs were posted where latrines were covered up, kitchen signs where leftovers, cans, and other refuse were buried. We also looked for any paper, any clothing, or any equipment left behind. My crew didn't have to assemble too early because our inspections didn't start until the regiment pulled out.

The people in the towns where we spent the nights were very good to us. The attitudes of non-soldiers had changed considerably since the declaration of war. We stopped the first night in Tallahassee, Florida. How we got permission to use a school building I don't know, but I found a library table, threw my bed roll on it, and went to sleep. The next morning, if the bugler blew his reveille, I didn't hear it, nor had I set an alarm clock. I finally was roused by giggles and laughter. I looked through the glass panel doors of the library and saw little heads watching the sleeping visitor.

I came to life. The teachers shooed the little ones away from the doors. I dressed and rolled my bed roll and I thought I would make a quick getaway, but one of the young teachers approached and said, "Lieutenant, my class hears the radio, sees the movies, and these days most of it is about soldiers. But none of them have ever seen a soldier up close in uniform. Will you please?"

35

What does one say to a class of fourth-graders? I do remember saying that soldiers get lonely and I would like it very much if they would write me. Just a little note. Sure enough about a month later I received an envelope just stuffed with letters from that class.

This first day of travel must have been a shakedown day, for we travelled only about 150 miles. On leaving Tallahassee, the Column Commander got serious about getting across Alabama, Mississippi, Louisiana, and half of Texas. From Tallahassee we rode until we got to Fortenbleu State Park close to Mandeville. I don't know how the other regiments made out (155th Infantry Mississippi and 167th Infantry Alabama), but the Louisiana Regiment (156th Infantry) was welcomed. I do not know who put out the information as to where we would stop, but there were two or three school buses waiting when the regiment came rolling in.

My detail, following the regiment, didn't leave until we had made all the inspections and corrections. However, in spite of the fact that we drove into the bivouac after dark, it didn't take long to find the school bus from Baton Rouge and to share hugs, kisses, cookies, cakes, and pies that mothers and wives had brought. A few of the fellows rode to Baton Rouge with the bus, and we picked them up as we came through the next day. From Tallahassee to Mandeville was our longest ride, about 335 miles to Camp Bowie, Texas. Consider that the speed of a military column has to be the speed of the slowest vehicle.

The third morning of our move, my detail watched the last of the regiment's vehicles move out. We inspected all the areas and did whatever cleaning and straightening up was necessary, and then we took off. It was a like going home for a little while. It was only seventy miles to Baton Rouge. We felt sad as we passed through but couldn't stop. We felt proud, for we were training to fight a war and here was the town—our home—that we were representing.

We didn't know where we would bivouac for the night, but we didn't think of that too much. We were enjoying Louisiana.

Above: Cleaning up the bivouac area.

We crossed Louisiana and went all the way to Houston. We arrived after dark and bivouacked in a park somewhere.

My next problem started in the morning.

That morning we were introduced to something that we had only just heard of before: a "Blue Norther." It is a wind that blows down across the midwestern plains. The Blue Norther makes you think that someone left the gate open in Canada and let all the cold out. A limb had broken the windshield out of my half-ton truck. There was no way to replace that windshield until after we arrived at Camp Bowie. We were going to be travelling northwest, and the wind was blowing southeast—which meant that we would be travelling into that Blue Norther all day long.

It had warmed up like spring before we left Florida, so we hadn't dressed in long underwear. The Blue Norther reminded us it was still winter. As we pulled out of Houston with no windshield, I wondered where I could find something else to cover up with. We were in wools and I did have one of those nice short camel-hair coats, but the wind was not very kind to us at all.

Above: Marie at Camp Bowie. Below: Camp Bullis, 1942. Note the WWI-style uniforms and equipment.

We were a little more lax about taking time to stop, buy coffee, and warm up.

■ ■ ■

We didn't like Camp Bowie on first sight, but it was a place where we could stop and get out of the wind. Our supporting town was Brownwood. It had a lot of plusses—not big but a lot of nice people.

Camp Bowie was built in a large circle, with the regiments facing the giant parade ground in the middle. The parade ground was so large it still had wild shrubs in the middle. The jackrabbits didn't know they were surrounded. During our breaks from close order drill, once in a while we would make a large circle with a jackrabbit in the middle to see if it could be caught. Nearly all of our soldiers were from Louisiana, so not many had seen a jackrabbit up close. The jackrabbits kept it that way. Not one was ever caught. It sounds funny to chase rabbits, but soldiers in their time off are easy to entertain. The nervous energy that is built up from working hard, training, and exercising makes them want to find something to do. Play baseball, enter the boxing programs, swim, chase rabbits, chase squirrels, make pets out of wild baby pigs, go to town.

Not long after we arrived at Camp Bowie, a lot of orders came down for individual officers. Many officers were sent to Fort Benning, the Infantry School of the Army. I received orders to report to a school called Junior Officers Training College at Camp Bullis, Texas: *Report 6/March/42 and end 19/April/42.* Camp Bullis was located about twenty miles north of San Antonio. I found that it was the "pet school" of General Walter Kruger, the Army Commander. General Kruger wanted his junior officers brought up professionally trained in leadership, squad, and platoon tactics, as well as in weapons.

Our Division Commander, General Persons, knew it was the Army Commander's pet school. We received our orders and the day before we departed Camp Bowie, all the junior officers going to Camp Bullis from the 31st Division found themselves standing on General Person's carpet. The General gave us a little pep talk and finished by saying, "All of you that do good at Camp Bullis, you will receive leave and a promotion." The General meant for us to show General Kruger how good the junior officers of the 31st Division were. The General sort of indicated that if we didn't do well, he could find us some special details when we got back.

After the year of training with Louisiana maneuvers and winter maneuvers in North Carolina, we were a cocky bunch and we didn't really believe that Camp Bullis would prove too much of a problem. We arrived at Camp Bullis, and the first officer who greeted us was a little, short mean-looking Colonel— and mean he was. He was the head instructor of the school, and when he shouted *"Jump!"* the only question was *"How high?"* We had very little classroom work. Nearly all of our instruction took place in the field. We were running, jumping, crawling, sliding, ducking, and hiding—day in and day out, cold, sun, and rain.

Part of our training area was in an old artillery impact area, where there were many old shells that had not exploded. We were often reminded not ever to roll one over because it might explode.

One morning we were marched out to our parade ground for a short lecture on aggressive fighting. We were lined up to form three sides of a square. The instructor had his back to the open side. He was hot into his lecture when a sad-looking private eased up behind him. Finally, the instructor became aware of him.

We could see the private and what he was carrying. Some of us were getting a little nervous. The instructor turned, and there the private was with an unexploded artillery shell in his hands. With some enthusiasm, he said, "Captain, I found that dud you wanted."

The Captain said, "I didn't want you to pick it up. I wanted you to mark it so we could get rid of it."

"But Captain, I got it; here it is."

The Captain said, "Don't shake it."

The private was getting nervous, and we already were. We were looking for a way to give the Captain and private more room to themselves. An axiom for staying alive is, "Don't monkey with unexploded artillery shells." The private began to bobble that dud, and finally lobbed it to the Captain. At the same time someone set off a quarter pound of dynamite.

When I raised my head, no one was still on his feet. We were all prone and trying to get smaller.

Instructors have a bad habit of thinking up little stunts like that to prove a point. The students don't usually forget.

Camp Bullis was not all bad. During the six weeks we were there, the powers that be were also running cooks' and bakers' schools. The cooks were supplied with ample and good supplies, and they didn't mind doing the best they could with it. Steaks, roasts, veggies of all kinds—and they were not too far from Louisiana to know how to cook rice and how to serve it. The best and biggest treats that came out of mess hall were from the bakers' school. With our Cajun cooks back at Camp Bowie we were usually served tasty food, but we had no bakers who could compare with this school's products. Delicious rolls, doughnuts, pies, and cakes were served not just at meal time. When we came in late from a field problem, coffee and baked goods were waiting for us. This made for *morale.*

■ ■ ■

Opposite: Van and Marie Roques Mayhall in their wedding portrait, April 25, 1942.

The Reception Went on Without Us

A surprise awaited me in San Antonio. I went in one weekend to see if I could find my father's brother. I had met him in 1927 when we all gathered to bury my grandfather, William Ambrose Mayhall. This brother was William Mayhall, Jr., and when I found a telephone book, his name popped out. I phoned Uncle Bill, and he greeted me like I was a long lost son. I got into town some way, and he picked me up and gave me the Cook's Tour of San Antonio. He also showed me around Pritchard Oil Company, of which he was the manager. It was not a big oil company; but considering that it was the only one I had ever been in, I was much impressed. Uncle Bill told me that nearly everything that Pritchard Oil Company could produce was going to the Army or Air Corps. Considering 2nd lieutenants were not familiar with the demands of the War Department, I thought sending everything to the Army and Air Corps was a nice gesture.

Uncle Bill took me over to meet Billie—William Mayhall III. When we grinned at each other we knew the same blood ran through us both. We liked each other from the start. Billie had a beautiful and pleasant wife named Joy. Joy put up with me. I spent a couple of weekends on their sofa.

Uncle Bill looked at me like he was looking at one of his younger brothers, Norris. Uncle "Not" had been in World War I. If my father ever thought I reminded him of his brother, he never mentioned it to me. Uncle Bill looked at me in a different light, as a young man studying to fight. I think when he was young Uncle Not was a little on the wild side. He was certainly no shrinking violet.

Marie got to looking for me while I was at Camp Bullis. She phoned when one of my friends was officer of the day, and he told her that I was in San Antonio at my cousin's house. Marie phoned Mother and got the information, and one Sunday morning Joy woke me up on the sofa and announced, "Marie wants to talk to you." This announcement had me at attention right away. I feared something awful had happened. We had last talked to each other in the middle of February and it was now mid-March. It was so good to hear her voice that I made plans to meet her in Houston the next weekend to talk about getting married.

Married.

I went back to Camp Bullis in new spirits. This beautiful girl whom I had loved since high school seemed interested in marrying me.

Back at Bullis I worked harder, studied harder, and did everything that I could do to be sure that I would get the grades that would get me promoted and a leave. A 2nd Lieutenant at that time was paid $125.00 per month. With a promotion to 1st Lieutenant I would be paid much more money—$152.00 a month. First Lieutenant's pay seemed to be comfortable enough to consider marriage.

The week zipped by. One of my brother officers who had a car was going to Houston for the weekend—my transportation there and back was no problem.

Marie and I met at the Rice Hotel, which was the only hotel that I knew by name in the city. It was a first-class hotel, and we both had nice rooms. We met with my father, and he took us to see the rooming house that he "layed over" in. Dad was a railroad man, a conductor on a train that ran from New Orleans, crossed the river at Baton Rouge, and then came to Houston. We told Dad what we were in Houston for.

There was a steak house across the street from the Rice Hotel called the Wagon Wheel, which was supposed to be the best in town. We went there for lunch. I don't know what we had to eat. I was mostly interested in Marie, sitting across the table from me. We had both matured so much over the fourteen months that we were apart, and now we were trying to make a lifelong decision. We made the decision in spite of the war or

Above: Norris (Uncle "Not") Mayhall (left) in WWI.

where I would be going. We said to each other, "Let's get married at the first opportunity." We were looking at the end of school at Camp Bullis, because I had been promised leave.

My brother officers came by the hotel Sunday afternoon. I climbed into the car, waved good-bye. I was in another world after our meeting, so it never occurred to me to wonder how Marie was going to get out of the hotel, get to the train, and get home by herself. Thank goodness Marie had never been one to wait around and be led.

The final two weeks at Camp Bullis didn't pass as quickly. We had field problems, night problems, and in-house lectures. The weather was warming up, and during the field problems I began to notice that, in this deer reserve where we were, there were a lot of ticks looking for warm blood. As we sat still and quiet under trees in cover, the ticks came out in platoon formation and climbed into our clothes looking for a nice spot to take a bite. We had tick-taking-off time when we got back to quarters. Ticks, when they find a place that satisfies them, get right with it, work their heads in until they have good bloodsucking depth, and go to work. They swell up to about ten times their original size. However, if we stuck the tick's backside with a smoldering cigarette, the tick abandoned its position and retreated. I managed to confuse the ticks pretty good. To me, it was still cold enough to wear longjohns, and the ticks had problems finding me.

Below: Husband and wife cut their wedding cake before rushing to the train station.

The last week of school passed by. On a Thursday the grades were posted—I received grades of excellent. I sent off a telegram to the colonel commanding our regiment asking for permission to get married and for ten days leave. Well, General Persons, our Division Commander, didn't kid around. I received the works: promotion to 1st lieutenant, ten days leave, and permission from Colonel Cuttner, Regimental Commander, to get married.

I phoned Marie that I was coming home to marry her. By the time I arrived, everything was in motion—but not the wedding itself. Everyone was glad to see me, but I mostly was invited to stay out of the way. There were showers, parties, dinners, and many plans. On the fourth day before I had to report back to Camp Bowie there was a rehearsal and dinner. The next day, Saturday, April 25, 1942, 8:00 A.M., we walked down the aisle of St. Joseph Church and were married.

Evelyn, Marie's younger sister, was her bridesmaid. C.A., my brother, stood for me as best man. Durward Babin sang "Ave Maria" for us. We left the church and went to Mama and Papa's for cake-cutting and a small, quick reception. My brothers-in-law served me drinks from both sides, giving me some very important instructions on how to get along as a married man. Marie and I had to catch the train leaving at 11:00 A.M., going to Houston on our way to Camp Bowie. The reception went on without us.

Our first stop on the way was Houston. Dad had arranged a hotel room close to the station and got the information we needed to get on another train Sunday going in the right direction. I don't know that either of us came to any great decisions during this train ride. We enjoyed each other's company, conversation, being near each other, and I supposed we dozed a little.

I had not been to Brownwood since going to Camp Bullis, and being as untrained to be a husband as I was, I had made no plans for a place to live for my wife and me. The Army had been taking care of me. They had let me sleep in tents, on the ground, in vehicles, under vehicles, in graveyards, and wherever, but made no plans for my wife. We arrived in Brownwood late in the

afternoon. I had never been in town before to know if there was
a hotel. The good Lord took over, and a nice lady took pity on our
situation as we wandered around asking about places to stay.
She asked us if we would like to come home with her. She had an
extra bedroom. Off we went. This was the best offer we had had.

The lady was very nice to us, took us home and showed us
the bedroom. It was nice—not palatial, but nice. I don't remember what we did about something to eat, but bedtime did arrive.
We changed into bed clothes and sat down on the bed and all
hell broke loose. The pieces of wood that held the box springs
and mattress gave way and down to the floor we went. I have
never heard so much noise in my life. After the noise, embar-
rassment set in. Newly married people breaking the bed—what
would the lady of the house think? The lady of the house came
and knocked on the door, and we explained that we had just sort
of sat down on the bed and it fell through. She grinned and
helped us put it back together and, thank goodness, it didn't
happen again.

The next day I reported for duty. I was assigned as an Executive Officer to A Company and found that I had a new commanding officer, Captain Pauley. We got along very well. I
didn't know much about being an executive officer, but I
worked at it.

After going to school one is supposed to know something. So,
my first job was to put on a demonstration of all the different
weapons in the division. The word went out, and the next Saturday the townspeople—all families and all wives—were
invited to come inspect us and the weapons. Our advertise-
ments were well received and a large showing came to look us
over.

Not very long after this happened, I was ordered to take
over the command of B Company as Acting Company Commander. So many of our officers were off at school or somewhere else,
we were lucky if there were two officers in a company, when
there were supposed to be six. At B Company I was the only officer for many weeks. When I got through signing for all the
sheets, pillowcases, rifles, bayonets, machine guns, mortars, pistols, tents, cots, jeeps, kitchen equipment, and all the other lit-

Above: Van Mayhall leading the Company in the Fourth of July parade.

tle things that the government lends to run a company, I felt pretty weighted down.

I looked at the Company and they looked at me. After all the signing was over the 1st Sergeant introduced me to them. I made my first and only speech to the Company. It was short. "I hate a liar and I hate a thief. If you get in trouble and tell me the truth, I will stand next to and behind you. If you steal from any of the men in my company, I will find you." And I did.

During this time the companies and battalions were going through corps proficiency tests. Not having any officers, I had to depend on my noncommissioned officers to carry the load. Thank goodness all of my noncommissioned officers were good and knew what they were doing. The battalion won the corps proficiency test. As a result, we were given the prize of marching in parades for the Fourth of July. People in Dallas and Tulsa had been asking for troops to march in their parades, and that turned out to be us.

We moved into an area between Dallas and Fort Worth and pitched our pup tents in military rows. Word came down that we could take our soldiers into town to find whatever entertainment was available. This was the night before the Fourth of July parade. The troops took advantage of this situation, and they did have a good time. The area around Camp Bowie was dry. That is, no beer, no whiskey—it didn't even rain.

It is a well-known fact that, after months of training, people in the Army and other services will have a beer or two, even a night full of imbibing, and will have a tendency to notice certain unkind remarks of any kind that may injure the pride and dignity of one's own outfit. Suddenly there are yells, shouts, fists being swung. Where there was peace and quiet, now there are people rolling around on the floor, tables upturned, bottles and glasses rolling all over. One wonders how it got started, and one wonders how it is going to get stopped. An MP whistle is the only thing that can arrest the attention of a fight. There is nothing but trouble to come from being picked up by the MPs. Much explaining has to be done by the offender as well as the CO.

I went around with the MPs seeking the people tearing up the town. As we arrived at one bar, an MP was getting up off of the floor. It seems that the MP had raised his night stick as if to strike one of my company men, and another one *sort of* caught his arm up in the air and *sort of* threw the MP over his shoulder and was *sort of* holding him down with one foot while holding one of his arms. When the men recognized me, everything got quiet. I suggested they get back to the convoy, which was fixing to leave. The MPs seemed to be satisfied to let everything slide.

The MPs told me that they were holding some people in jail. I took the convoy back to camp and I told my 1st Sergeant, Orien Robichaux, that I had to go back and get someone out of jail. Sergeant Robichaux wanted to go with me, and away we went. When we got to the MP headquarters, we found an old cavalry Major storming around, mad as a wet hen. He had been disturbed at a cocktail party, and without too much looking we could see that he was slightly in his cups. I told him I was the Company Commander of these people who had been disrupting his town and his party. He had me standing at attention and accused me of trying to take over his town and beating up his MPs and wrecking the party places. He said after winding down a little bit that he would report me to the Commanding General of the 31st Infantry Dixie Division.

He paused for breath at that point, which gave me a chance to speak, and I suggested that he report me to General Persons. I would tell General Persons that he stood me at attention and chewed me out in front of my enlisted man, and that I recognized that he had come to his headquarters straight from a drinking party. Berating an officer in front of enlisted men was a no-no, especially a Company Commander. The Major quieted down, invited me into his office, and was much more cordial. The final and most important part of the situation was we got out without anyone being arrested. I got my people out of jail and we all went back to camp happy, thinking we were about even with the MPs who had worked some of our people over.

The parade went off fine. We had all broken out the best khaki uniforms we had, and the men were happy to see the sidewalks and windows full of people looking, shouting, and waving. Some of the men were happy to see some of those same MPs from the night before directing traffic for us.

We went on to Tulsa and the only thing I remember was that we were well received. I was well received on a personal basis because of my name. There were some Mayhalls in oil in Tulsa and they were the only Mayhalls I had ever heard of that had been on the receiving end of that Black Gold. I was wined and dined by people whose names I never knew before or since.

After our "prize" of marching in parades in Dallas and Tulsa, we returned to Camp Bowie. We went back to the combat ranges and practiced shooting pop-up targets. We had been supplied with jeeps and the drivers had to be taught to keep them in shape. More rifle training, now with the M-1 Garand, which fired semi-automatic from an eight-round clip. More machine-gun fire, more pistol, more bayonet drills, and more creeping and crawling.

■　■　■

Midsummer 1942

*I*n midsummer of 1942 we sped up all of our activities. We hadn't kept up with the War news too much, so it came as a surprise when one 4 A.M. we got the orders: "Bring all machine guns and all Browning automatic rifles and turn them in to the S-4 Supply for boxing and shipping to England."

The Germans had run the British armies out of France at Dunkirk two years before. The Germans had nearly wiped out the force the British had sent to throw them back and keep them from taking over France and Holland. This was the first indication how serious the Germans were and how good they were at making war.

They completely overran France and chased the British and Canadians out into the English Channel. Britain called for help from its citizens: Anyone with a boat that could cross the English Channel went to pick up soldiers who were being backed into the water. Fishing boats, yachts, ferry boats—all went to save as many soldiers as possible from being killed or captured.

The weapons lost at this Dunkirk—the cannons, tanks, trucks, machine guns, automatic rifles, and records—were countless. The loss in equipment was a terrible expense, but the most important need was to get the soldiers out, get them off French soil and back to England where their wounds and mental health could be mended. Three hundred eighty thousand allied troops were ferried out by all kinds of boats. This happened between May 26 and June 3, 1940. The British, two years later, hadn't been able to catch up. Their war industry was doing all it could, and the Germans were doing all they could by bombing British cities.

In spite of the stepped-up training that I had been thrown into, Marie and I saw each other regularly. Marie would come to camp and eat with me in the Officer's Mess. Sometimes it would be too late to go back into town by herself, and we would spend the night on my one-person cot in my little Company Commander tent. Many times Marie had to eat by herself, go back to our room in town by herself, find laundry and stores with no help. With the time I had to spend out in the field training day and night, Marie spent a lot of time alone.

One day Marie said to me, "I want to go home."

She said, "I want to see if Mama and Papa are all right." Marie didn't indicate that I was spending too much time with Company B, nor did she say she was lonely. She just said, "I have to see Mama and Papa." And she left.

We didn't have a car. I had never tried to buy one. There didn't seem to be a big need for a car with the amount of time I had to spend at camp. Somehow Marie got home. I think maybe my wife wondered if her husband was all right, because it didn't take long for her to come back—about four days I think. I was very glad to see her back.

In the meantime, B Company was digging defensive positions, watching tanks run over the holes we had dug to let us know we were somewhat safe if we dug deep enough and stayed in the foxhole. Instructions never indicated what to do if the hole caved in on you. Junior officers and noncommissioned officers trained in map reading. After we worked in the classroom over our maps and compasses, it was time to go into the field.

Now, for some reason, going into the field to run compass problems does not usually take place in the daytime. I divided my sergeants and corporals into teams and assigned compass courses to each group. We went out at sunset and let each group off the truck about three quarters of a mile apart. The compass courses were designed so that they would not cross each other, but they would all come together at the end of the courses. At the top of a small hill we planned to meet and have coffee. That

Above: Married but often apart—not an uncommon situation for a young couple in 1942—Marie and Van exchanged many photographs of each other.

is, we would meet if they read their compasses right and didn't get lost out in the woods.

My jeep driver, 1st Sergeant, and I went to the little hill and waited. I sent the jeep and driver back to camp to pick up the coffee. The 1st Sergeant and I thought it would be a good idea to build a fire on top of the hill to keep the teams from going by their final point. We began gathering wood, got a small fire going. I reached down to pick up a piece of wood and something bit me on the hand. It stung so bad that I was sure I was in for a bad time. My whole hand began to throb.

I thought of snakes first, but there was no thrashing around in the grass. Spiders and scorpions and goodness knows what else went through my mind. The First Aid Station was about five miles away. The jeep was gone. I didn't think that I could run to the station. It would just make the poison or whatever move faster, so I calmed down and wondered what was going to happen now. I waited and watched my hand. The sting began to die down on its own. I never found out what bit me.

Our compass course teams began to come in. Some had to be called in, but for the most part they did good.

■   ■   ■

July 1942 sped by. Marie and I were beginning to adjust to being married. We loved each other and spent as much time together as we could. There were times when I managed to get to our room at the end of the day, but I would be nearly out on my feet. When Marie opened the door for me, I would just fall into the room. The field work we were doing and the schedules we were keeping did not leave much time for anything or anybody. Day maneuvers ran into nights. Night maneuvers ran into days. August 1942 was rushing along, and there wasn't a single let-up.

If you were not involved with the company for a battalion or regimental problem, Company Commanders were working with their noncoms. We worked on the sand (terrain) tables. We went to the combat ranges to work on the best ways to use terrain— how to use folds, rolls, ditches, and valleys in advancing, shooting, and defending. I begged, borrowed, and sometimes went a little further to get ammunition to get more time and practice on the combat ranges.

Then one day the Regimental Commander told me that his wife was going home and that I could have the apartment he and his wife had been using. The bedroom was large and upstairs with windows all around, and had a bathroom shared by only one other couple. The landlady had a large attic fan, so in the heat of the night everyone had to be very careful to keep their windows down far enough for the landlady to get some of the air being pulled through the house by the attic fan. Marie enjoyed finally having someone to talk to. The wife in the other young couple was alone about as much as Marie was.

■ ■ ■

Rumors

*L*ate in August, the rumors began to drift around: "We are going to move." "We are going overseas." "We as a regiment will be detached from our division." "We are going west." "We are going east." Everything got real serious when the insurance forms and "will" forms came down from Regiment to be filled out. All these young people, including me, had never had any idea we would need any insurance, much less a will. We were just coming out of a big depression, and the most money we had ever seen was right there on active duty. Parents didn't spend money on insurance, why should we? The insurance officer had his job cut out for him. However, the wills didn't cost anything, so in the end it wasn't hard to convince each soldier that it would be nice that Father, Mother, Brother or Sister could have whatever had been earned in the Army if anything happened to him.

Security was very tight. All leaves were cancelled. The Battalion and Company Commanders were called in by the Regimental Commander. The Regimental Commander stressed the fact that we were at war, that any moves we made would not be public information. If you could get away without telling your wife, don't tell her. It might save your life.

> *The Regiment (156th Infantry) will leave Camp Bowie, Texas, shortly. You will start preparing your units for movement to a port of embarkation. The other two regiments of the 31st Division will stay here.*

As we packed to leave, Marie asked where we were going. I said I didn't know—and I did not, even after we were on a rolling train. Marie told me that she thought she knew; some of the wives had been at the depot where the equipment was being loaded, and they had seen the address on boxes: "Fort Dix, New Jersey."

On September 15, 1942, we entrucked to go to Brownwood to entrain (as the military likes to say). I had never experienced anything like this before. The station was full of men, wives, and children. The children were crying, the wives wanted to go with us to the next camp. It grew more dramatic as more soldiers climbed on the train. It was close to midnight, and thoughts of whether or not we would ever see each other again slipped into our minds. There were many tears. I stood on the bottom step of the coach and waved good-bye to Marie as long as I could see her.

We stopped only to change train crews. The tracks were open all the way. I noticed we were travelling north nearly all the time. I wasn't surprised when we heard the conductor announce, "Chicago." We stopped long enough to get a hot meal and straighten our legs, then away we went. We arrived at Fort Dix on September 20. My first impression was that it was a beautiful place, but the barracks they moved us into looked like they had been occupied by wild men and surely hadn't been cleaned up before they departed.

We started cleaning as if we were going to stay. Showdown inspections started the day after arrival. We were short a lot of clothes. After riding the train for five days and cleaning up the camp on the sixth day, we finally got a bath. Bathing gets to be important. After so many days without a shower, everybody smells the same, but everybody stinks the same, too.

On September 22 we were moved out of the place we had cleaned up and put in tents. At this point it should have occurred to us that we were not to be detained here for very long. We were so busy that thinking was one of the things for which we didn't have too much time. Everyone had to have a new round of shots. Everyone had to turn in their nice-fitting wool clothes and be issued sets of impregnated wools which were supposed to protect us from gas. This was done in another all-night operation. Taking up clothes and issuing pants and shirts by size is a long and tedious job, so at times even the Company Commander (me) was helping to get supplies to the men.

September 24 ended with a regimental warning order, "The Regiment will move September 25, 1942." Every order was issued on a need-to-know basis. The warning order did not tell us, but we would ride down to New York, detrain, and walk with all our equipment to board a British ship, wave good-bye, and salute the Statue of Liberty.

From New York we would sail up the coast toward Halifax, Canada, where we would join the rest of a convoy going to Europe.

■ ■ ■

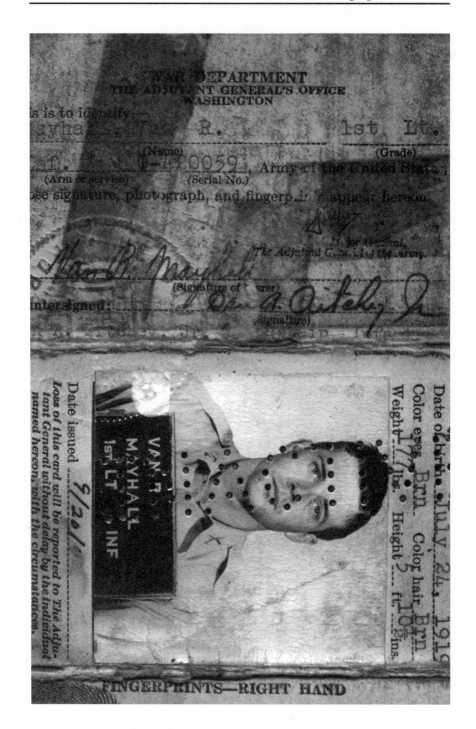

Opposite: Identification papers: Van Mayhall's visa.

Consolidated Mess

*W*e were far enough out to sea to test the guns. The ship was equipped with 20mm cannons, 40mm Bofors, and one 8-inch gun mounted on the fantail that was the only gun with a special crew. The 20mm and Bofors cannons were operated by the trained machine-gunners among the troops. So Sunday morning the gunners were on the weapons and balloons were released as targets and the 20mm Hotchkiss began howling away, and the 40mm Bofors Ack-Ack began their *boom-boom-boom*.

Many of us watched the firings; another large group was at the first Catholic Mass since before leaving Camp Bowie, kneeling for prayers. One of my officers, Lieutenant Roland Champagne, had decided to sleep in. He was awakened by the gun drills.

Lieutenant Champagne poked his head out of his room door. There was a large burst of fire, and he couldn't see anyone in the hall. His first thought was that we were under attack. They must be shooting at a German submarine! He closed his door, got one leg in his pants, one arm in his shirt, and he came out running, up the hall toward the big off-duty lounge. The lounge was empty. He quickly determined that everyone was at their lifeboat stations. This was serious! He pulled open a door, and there were all these people kneeling. He bumped his way in, telling them, "Let somebody in that *knows* how to pray!" He was sure we were sinking.

It took quite a while for his brother officers to forget Lieutenant Champagne's Sunday morning.

■ ■ ■

We arrived in the great inland harbor of Halifax and met the rest of the convoy that we would be part of. Our escort was made up of many warships of one kind or another. There were little ships, big ships, middle-size ships. The tin-can boats sped along on the outside of the convoy. Now and then one would come plowing through the convoy on the way to a radio alert that a German sub had been sighted. On our trip to Halifax there were supposed to have been two confirmed submarine kills. The German submarines liked to prowl up and down the eastern U.S. coast and into the Gulf of Mexico.

The convoy steamed out of Halifax Harbor about as soon as we arrived. Where the Germans had placed their spies and were getting their intelligence we never knew, but it was important not to stay in one place long. The longer we stayed in Halifax, the more probable the information would get to Germany that a big fat convoy was leaving loaded with troops, ammunition, tanks, trucks, gasoline, and rations.

We went scooting out into the ocean. On my ship, the 156th Infantry was packed in pretty tight, along with hospital troops and some other small units. The officers had it very good. For meals we were assigned to an eight-place table and there we were served breakfast, lunch, and dinner by waiters in white coats. The meals were excellent. To a bunch of infantry officers who had eaten most of their meals in the dark, standing up, sitting on anything handy, and a lot of time wondering what we were eating, this sitting at a table with linens, three forks, two knives, napkins, and at least two glasses was a real high-class experience.

I don't know how many officers became seasick. Only one at our table did. We ragged him so bad that he was over it in a couple of days.

We officers had state rooms. I shared mine with one other person. On a British ship, there was a big difference between what the officers got and what everyone else had. The enlisted men were packed in down belowdecks like sardines. They were

Above: Belowdecks shipboard, men sleep in bunks stacked floor to ceiling. (FDR Library)

assigned to beds (if you could call them that!) stacked from floor level to the ceiling, at least eight beds high stacked two feet above each other. Air circulation was not so good. Belowdecks more soldiers became seasick, and if your upstairs buddy got sick and began to upchuck, anyone below was in danger. With the ventilation as it was and the continuous cooking smells, the whole belowdecks was not that great for the weaker stomachs. The switch from Louisiana cooks and French cooking to English cooks and English cooking was one more reason why a lot of our Louisiana regiment lost weight on our crossing of the Atlantic Ocean.

Our ship was a good ship and fairly fast. Had we been by ourselves, the *Ontreses,* part of the British Orient line, would have made the crossing much faster than we did. However, convoy speed is as fast as the slowest ship, and then there was the zigzagging of the whole convoy trying to throw off the German submarines. If any ships were attacked, they were far enough away in the convoy that we did not see or hear.

Dodging enemy action did not help conditions belowdecks. There was only so much time to feed the troops, clean up after them, and only so much space for all of this to be done. There were only so many toilets and urinals, so that troops had to stand in line. Goodness knows how bad the systems worked when everyone had dire need for upchucking. It was like a big wreck on the highway—everything starts backing up, tempers flare, horns start blowing, and people want to be some other place.

People read whatever they could find. There were card games going on, and some of the biggest craps games I ever saw. There were other things that had to be done. Number one was lifeboat drills. We had to learn how to get to the lifeboats that we were supposed to be on to get off of that ship if need be. There was roll call every morning. There was exercising, trying to keep a little of the condition everyone came onto the boat with. There was map reading. We were going into the war zone, so learning aircraft identification was becoming more important.

Each day out meant we were closer to a country that had been pounded by German aircraft for some time. The Germans were so angry and frustrated when they found that the British were not going to allow them to invade England that they did as much damage as possible to the English cities.

The aircraft identification came home to everyone when there was an Air Alert on the 3rd of October, three days out from England. Everyone raced to their posts. The gunners and ammunition men uncovered their guns, broke out ammunition, and were ready for someone to say, "Fire." Our gunners were hunched down behind their guns tracking a big four-motored plane and wanting to shoot. But the all clear was sounded. Of course, there was a big sigh of relief. The English people with long-range field glasses knew immediately that this plane was a British Lancaster used for antisubmarine patrol. The Americans had never seen a Lancaster, but I think more than one decided to take aircraft identification a little more seriously.

We were closing on England, but still in dangerous waters. We felt relieved to see a flight of Spitfires come out to meet the convoy. By this time even the Americans knew what a Spitfire looked like. Spitfires were one of the fighter aircraft that shot down so many German fighters and bombers that the Germans would have to give up the idea of subduing the British by air.

The last days on the *Ontreses* were rather pleasant for everyone except the people who suffered from motion sickness. As we approached England, the sea began to roll. The waves must have been twenty to twenty-five feet. The front end of the liner would dip down and then come up on the next wave. I was enjoying it. Sergeant Robichaux was not. He had been sick all the way across. Nothing about this boat trip agreed with him— the rolling of the boat, the quarters, the English food, the sight of the latrines. He managed to hold down Hershey Bars. He said that was what got him to England.

We landed at Bristol on October 6. We didn't like the smell there, either. We asked some English soldiers what the stink was and, of course, they had to have some fun with the new troops. So they told us, "It's just some of them dead Germans we shot down." Well, stink or no stink, we had to get off that boat and get some other place. A nice fat ship full of troops makes a good target.

Off the ship onto the British lorries, and we were taken to Spring Hill. It was a beautiful place as far as scenery, hills, and valleys, but the wrong time of year for us because it was cold, windy, and raining a rain which seemed to go right through us.

Here we were in jolly old England. Our equipment had not arrived yet. We were unpacking, cleaning, and working out some kind of training schedule. We didn't like the setup. It was our first experience with consolidated mess. The whole battalion ate in one mess hall, with English cooks and English food cooked the way the English cook. We preferred our own cooks from Louisiana. We were introduced to a new form of mattresses—the English called them *palasais*. We called them a sack full of straws. This was one of the things that kept the company busy for a while—filling sacks full of straw to sleep on. Under this straw mattress was a nice piece of plywood that

would send you back a couple of times to the straw pile to be
sure you had enough straw between you and that wood.

Army business soon got back on track—the lectures, the
drilling, the exercising, and the long marches. It seemed to be a
normal part of a hike for the weather to turn to rain, cold, and
wind.

I got off the post on the weekends. The weather seemed to
change just getting off of that hill. I went to a little town called
Broadway, where there was a small hotel called the Legend
Arms. It looked like it had been built about the time Columbus
discovered America. It was warm. The fireplaces were large
enough to stand up in. I had occasion to spend the night there
and was introduced to something I had never seen nor heard of.

I went to the assigned room, got into my PJs and was fixing
to crawl into bed. There was a knock on the door. I went to the
door, opened it, and there was a maid with something that
looked like a big copper frying pan with a long handle. She
brushed by me and went to my bed and began to run this big

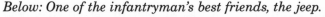

Below: One of the infantryman's best friends, the jeep.

frying pan around under the sheets. I was finally told that there were hot coals in the frying pan, and she was warming the sheets. I didn't think so much of it until I crawled into the sack and the bed was warm as toast. I guessed it was an idea they forgot to bring over on the Mayflower.

It was about this time that orders came down to send six soldiers with all of their equipment to Headquarters. These men were to be transferred to one of the American units that was headed for the invasion of Africa. I felt so bad about this move for these men; they had been with B Company for nearly two years. It was like sending them away from home. These men were not the brightest, smartest, and best-trained men we had; they were the ones we would have gotten rid of if we could. Still, I was sorry, because I felt that they had been put in harm's way without the rest of us.

■ ■ ■

Tea With Captain Churchill

*T*he week wore on and Sunday came, and we were not
doing anything but taking it easy. Then, some guy comes
into the quarters hollering, "Anybody want to go to tea?" Well,
there were a lot of men who would have been glad to go for coffee or beer, but not too many south Louisiana officers would
give you thanks for a cup of tea. The officer asking for tea
drinkers was a liaison officer, whose job it was to help see that
all of the troops coming off of boats got to where they were supposed to go, and see that they were supplied with what they
needed.

So, I said, "I'll go. I like tea." We always had tea at home.
Mother loved it. On with the best uniform and into his jeep and
away we went. As we took off, I asked where we were going.

He said, "Stow-on-the-Wold."

I said, "'Stow-on-the-Wold'? Where in the hell is that?"

He said, "Just a short way down the road."

We came over the top of a hill and down between two stone
fences. They were high enough that I couldn't see too much on
either side. We came to a turn, and Captain Liaison Officer
announced, "Stow-on-the-Wold."

It was not a very impressive place. There were a few stone
houses with straw roofs. We went a little past the town and
turned into a driveway between two large grey stone posts.
About half a mile down was a great big grey stone mansion, to
the left a broad field sloping up to the woods, and there were
deer feeding. We crossed what we might call a bayou at home. It
would be a moat here in England.

71

Above: Captain Mayhall (center) with fellow B Company members Lieutenants Songy and Albriton in October 1942.

We stopped in front of the big double doors, got out, and knocked. The door was opened by a well dressed servant. Captain Liaison Officer identified himself; he was expected. We were invited in and then we waited for the master of the house. When the master of the house arrived, he shook hands with the liaison officer, and I was introduced to Captain Churchill, the Prime Minister's brother. Captain Churchill was long retired, but still doing what he could do, keeping the big old estate together.

This was my first experience with English tea. I didn't know biscuits, jelly, rolls, and a number of other tasty eatables came with it! Captain Churchill was very interested in the new American arrivals. I was questioned about being from Louisiana with an English-type, Welsh-type name. After tea, he took us for a tour of the mansion. We walked into a great hall as big as a gymnasium where there were three tiers of paintings, large and small, all beautiful. At the end of the giant hall was the Prime Minister's favorite, a picture of lions with bright and beautiful colors.

My mind was so full after this experience that I don't really remember any of the trip back to the camp. I didn't try to explain to anyone where I had been nor whom I had met.

We got to visit around a little more. It was a real surprise that we visited Chippin Camden in Stratford-on-Avon, which was Shakespeare's home. I didn't get to visit the theater where his plays were presented, but I was impressed with just seeing the old buildings. Our principal at Catholic High, Brother Peter, thought so much of and had so much respect for the writings of Shakespeare that he came to our class and read the plays to us. We enjoyed them, and I remembered those plays about history and war, eight years later sitting on Shakespeare's doorstep, though I hadn't read a line of them since high school.

■ ■ ■

Trading Rifles for Pencils

I was occupied with Company training, trying to get a handle on what we would train for, where we would train. We were going through the same things as always, marching, hiking. We wandered around as if we were in a new house looking out the windows to see what we could see. The important thing was to keep everybody busy.

On October 20, rumors began bubbling from many different directions. Sure enough, the next day word came down for me to report to Cheltenham to receive special orders. Before I left, I issued warning orders to my officers and First Sergeant that we would probably be moving shortly after I came back.

Cheltenham was the big headquarters for the G-4 ETOUSA (European Theater of Operations United States of America); this was the headquarters for anything that moved. If there were any piece of equipment, tanks, planes, half-tracks, cannons, rifles, pistols, uniforms, shoes, rations, or anything else that you can imagine that soldiers would need, this headquarters had a piece of paper to say where it's going, to whom it's going, when it's going, when it will get there, and how many of it.

We were greeted at the Cheltenham Headquarters by a Major Goodman, whom I have never seen again. He gave me instructions for B Company. We had been in England two weeks waiting to find out what we were supposed to do; now it was hurry up and get there. We went back to Spring Hill, and thank goodness I had passed the warning order. This cut down on the amount of time it took to get everything ready to move. We worked all night and we entrucked and moved out early on the next day for someplace called Tidworth. We arrived at Tidworth in the late afternoon, and it began to dawn on me what had happened: B Company had been assigned to run a Quartermaster Depot, QM-124.

I reported to a Lieutenant Colonel Gent, my new Commanding Officer. He offered me a cigar and showed me where my office was, and explained that the British who were running QM-124 would pull out at the end of the week. This meant, "You and your Company have a week to learn how to run this Quartermaster Depot." My people had been training to be infantry soldiers! All we had to do was to turn some riflemen and machine-gunners into typists, checkers, warehousemen, and a few other specialists we didn't know anything about yet. In the States, spend two years in the field, sun, rain, heat, cold, sand. Overseas, lay down rifles to pick up pencils and typewriters!

We had to take bills of lading and load trucks with rations to go to the different outfits that we had to supply, but didn't know where the outfits were. My Motor Corporal normally had two jeeps to take care of; now, he had twenty-five $2\frac{1}{2}$-ton trucks to oil, gas, repair, and keep on the road. His question to me was, "Captain, where do we get wrenches and tools to work on these trucks? We don't even have an air compressor."

Everyone at my Headquarters and the two platoons pitched in and went to work. They could see that working inside beat the hell out of long marches and mud. In addition, we were all eating better. The men found that if they put an elbow in the right place a crate of special food would fall off a stack, break open, and couldn't be shipped. So this food would have to be turned over to our kitchen crew instead of letting it spoil. A coffee roasting unit had been turned over to our use, and if there is one thing South Louisiana boys know how to do, it's how to roast coffee beans, grind them, and bag them; and they certainly know how to drip it into the best coffee one ever tasted.

Lieutenant Colonel Gent called me in and suggested that I write and practice a defense plan for the QM Depot. I couldn't see any need for ground defense in the middle of England, but there could be a sneak air attack. I went to work, looked over

Above: On review in Cheltenham, England. The small inked-in arrow just right of center points to Captain Mayhall.

the ground. We were in a bowl with rolling hills around us. I picked some places for machine guns and places for automatic rifles to support the machine guns, and spread the rifle men around where I thought they would do the most good. We practiced enough times to know where to scatter to if the air raid sirens were to go off. I wrote it up and gave it to Lieutenant Colonel Gent, and he seemed pleased.

Not being used to staff work, I was a little shocked the next day when the order came out exactly as I had written it, but without my name anywhere on it.

Whenever Colonel Gent felt like checking up on everybody, he would sound a practice alert to see everybody come running out of their places of work. Cooks, mechanics, typists, warehousemen, and drivers grabbed helmets, rifles, ammunition, and gas masks, turned back into infantrymen, and ran for their emplacements.

In fact, the Germans were making quite a few sneak attacks, nuisance raids. On October 30, the air raid sirens went off four times. B Company went scrambling to our defensive positions, but we saw and heard nothing.

Only two of Company B platoons were at Tidworth. Lieutenant Champagne and 3rd Platoon were at Exeter running an overflow QM depot. Lieutenant Logan, Lieutenant Hack, and 2nd Platoon were sent to Taunton, where they were handling all the maintenance and transport for a large motor pool.

These two platoons had the same problems that we were having at Tidworth. The people who had been running the depot at Exeter and the motor pool at Taunton pulled out only a short time after the B Company platoons arrived. Considering that some of the infantrymen hadn't been old enough to drive before they came into the service, it was a fast-training program to get them into condition to handle large trucks on the "wrong" side

Below: Capt. Mayhall (left) with B Company Lieutenants Spencer, Albriton, Champagne, Hack, and Songy.

of the road. I never knew how many fender-benders there were, but no one was broken up, thank goodness.

At Exeter, it was just a matter of work and sweat, loading trucks from box cars and unloading the trucks into storage. One of the things that this platoon had to learn about warehousing was to be able to find what they unloaded when it was called for. If ten days of rations have been put in front of fifty cases of rifles and rifles are ordered, the rifles can't be loaded without moving ten days of rations.

Already the end of October was here, which meant that I would have to go back to Regimental Headquarters at Spring Hill, find the regimental pay officer, and collect all the money to pay B Company. We hadn't been paid since we left Camp Bowie, which meant a little jingling money would be very welcome. It came as a shock on our first payday overseas to see that the American dollar was not on the schedule, but British pounds and shillings would be issued. Now we had something else to learn—how much does everything cost in British money? It shocked me when the Finance Officer just threw a sack on a scale and said, "This is your change," but he did count the bills. One company payroll is a lot of money, so I as a Payroll Officer had to wear my .45 loaded.

I loaded B Company's money and started on the 160 miles to pay everybody. I went to Tidworth first, and then headed for the 3rd Platoon at Exeter. From Tidworth I had to go south across the Salisbury Plain where, I had read, knights had done some jousting. At Salisbury, I turned west and headed for Exeter. The countryside was beautiful. It took me a long time to finally realize that the same Gulf breeze whipped around in the Gulf of Mexico, crossed the Atlantic Ocean, and blew on England, keeping it at a moderate temperature.

I arrived at Exeter and called the 3rd Platoon together. They were very happy to see me, not because of my wonderful attributes as a Company Commander but because I was bringing the money. They had had none of any kind of money since we left Camp Bowie. Lieutenant Champagne was glad to see me because he had been working in a vacuum. It's helpful to the

Above: 25 November 1942 V-Mail with censor's stamp of approval. As the holidays approached, soldiers' letters home dwelled on thoughts of reuniting with their families.

morale of an outfit to have a little bit of information about what is going on. He wanted to know what was happening to the rest of the Regiment, so I filled him in as much as possible. Second Battalion was to be detached from the Regiment and would go to Africa with the African invasion. We were supposed to get another battalion when available from the States. And A Company would go to where they would be part of a Combat Landing School. All of the troops that would hit the beaches in France would hit them first at this school.

In this school the units came in on assault boats, opposed by machine-gun fire (blanks), antipersonnel mines, and concrete pill boxes with machine guns. The assault people came ashore and moved into position to blow gaps in the razor-wire fences, with supporting fire trying to keep the pill boxes buttoned up and the machine-gunners' heads down until they could be knocked out.

The 3rd Battalion would be school troops for the Assault School. C Company had gone to Birmingham. Service Company was sent to London. What happened to Cannon Company, the Regiment's heavy weapons company, I don't know, unless they were part of Assault School backup. D Company was part of a Heavy Weapons School somewhere.

Assault School proved to be something that we could not be careless with. Some time later, troops were climbing down the side of ships on rope ladders. Someone forgot that there was a war going on and not enough security had been set up. German E-boats, similar to our PT-boats, slipped in and sank several vessels at the cost of well over seven hundred soldiers and sailors.

After swapping information with Lieutenant Champagne, he suggested I should go down to Plymouth and see what the Germans had done there. Well, I was too close not to go, so away I went. There was never a German on the ground at Plymouth unless his bomber was shot down, but the whole center of the town was completely gutted. It must have been a real hell there, with the bombs falling and the fires burning. We had often seen the fires and bomb damage that the Germans did to London, but we didn't often see what had been done to other cities. I left

Plymouth with a little more resolution than I had ever had before. I continually talked to members of the company to impress upon them what we were in England for.

■ ■ ■

I drove on to Taunton and was very satisfied to find Lieutenant Logan and Lieutenant Hack and the 2nd Platoon in good shape. This platoon had probably fallen into the best situation. Their quarters were good. Their mess was putting out good food, and nobody had broken legs or been sick. I took off for Tidworth by way of Bristol, Bath where the Romans had built bathhouses, on to Chippenham, through Marlborough, and south to Tidworth.

Strange things happen while a Company Commander is away, and usually a C.C. doesn't like it. Most of the time the C.C. would rather be at the company when it's inspected. A Lieutenant Colonel by the name of Kernuble had come up from Salisbury to inspect B Company. Everything was fine until he got to the garbage cans. He found some pork fat cut off of those special boxes that couldn't be shipped. Sergeant Landry, the Mess Sergeant, said he thought the inspector was going to throw a fit. He commenced to lecture the Mess Sergeant about throwing away perfectly good meat, and ended up by telling him, "My wife back in the States would love to have a piece of meat like you've thrown in the garbage."

My Mess Sergeant had always been helpful, cooperative, and did most anything for an inspecting officer (regardless of whether he was a jackass or not). So, Sergeant Landry offered to wrap him up a few pieces of that fat so the Lieutenant Colonel could take them with him. Somehow, the Inspecting Officer didn't quite see any humor in this offer. By the time the Lieutenant Colonel got through with his lecture, everybody within a half block around knew he was not pleased.

A few days after I got back to Tidworth, I learned about another little episode. There was a pub called the White Horse, and it was a nice, quiet little place to go sip a few bitters and shoot the bull. Well, some of B Company noncoms liked that little pub, and there was another faction that also liked the pub: British paratroopers. My B Company noncoms were sitting around a table one night enjoying stories past and present, when a paratrooper began to sing at the bar. How long he sang before he was noticed, I don't know, but one of the B Company people threw a big English penny across the floor in the direction of the singer. It was surprising how loud the sound of the penny bouncing across the floor was. Everybody in the pub seemed to hear it. The singer didn't think this was a compliment.

The British paratrooper picked up the coin and walked slowly across to the table and asked, "Who threw the penny?"

Webb, one of the B Company bunch, stood up and said, "I did." In a blink of an eye, the paratrooper hit him, and in another blink of an eye there were paratroopers popping up from everywhere. You didn't want to get into a fight with the British. They didn't back down—in a pub brawl or in battle. It didn't take long before these representatives from B Company were being bounced out of that pub and into the street.

Before they were tossed out of the pub, B Company didn't do bad. They had stirred the White Horse like it had never been stirred before. Tables turned over, chairs tumbled around, beer bottles rolled all over the floor—to say nothing of American infantrymen and British paratroopers rolling about the floor. It took a few days before the residue of the pub brawl disappeared: the black eyes, skinned knuckles, and the red welts. However, the look of pride that showed up in some of these soldiers lasted longer—that little sheepish look that said, "They wasn't so tough!"

■ ■ ■

Security Company, General Lee

*I*n spite of the fact that B Company had learned all they could from the British soldiers who were running QM-124 before we got there, there were still problems. I had to do something about those $2\frac{1}{2}$-ton trucks that we had fallen heir to. My Motor Corporal was doing his best with what he had. Americans of the WWII generation had given up filling a truck tire with a hand pump. We needed an air compressor. We needed a few more tools than a screwdriver and pair of pliers. So I packed up for another few days on the road and took off. I first went to Birmingham, where C Company was. I had been moving around more than they had, and had information to swap. They were ready to help me when I finished with the news. Someone turned up with a whole set of wrenches, still in their cases, and donated them to me when I promised: I would bring them back if they needed them, yes, yes, yes. They also mentioned that there was a big depot nearby.

I was running around England in a seven-seater, 21-horsepower Woolsley automobile. The engine could hardly pull it going uphill, but it did very well going down. I drove my Woolsley into the large depot warehouse. The Woolsley made me look a little bit more important than the ordinary Joe who came in a jeep. A sergeant greeted me, and I inquired about tools. I turned around and saw a beautiful air compressor, and I knew it had enough power to do our job back at Tidworth. I asked the sergeant who it belonged to, and he said, "Captain, I don't know."

I said to him, "That must be the one I was sent to get. Will you help me put it into the trunk of my Woolsley?" and he answered, "Yes, Sir."

When I returned to Tidworth and showed my mechanics what I had brought home, they thought I was some kind of hero. They retired the bicycle pump in a hurry when they heard that nice compressor kick off.

I met a British flight officer in one of the pubs, and of course we got around to talking about airplanes. The British were just as curious about us as we were about them, so I enjoyed the conversation, and in addition got an invite to go up in a plane the next day. I was hoping for something like a Mosquito or a two-seat Spitfire; however, that was not to be. This flight officer was testing the oldest bomber on the British list of military planes. It looked like a buzzard; its nose stuck far out with a machine gun bubble sticking down; the wings were long and wide and looked like they would flap in flight.

The flight officer didn't offer any suggestions as to where I should sit; so I wandered up front and climbed into the forward gun turret and went for the ride. On landing, my host said to me, "I say, Yank, the next time you go up, don't get into the forward turret. These planes have problems on landing and take-off and sometimes come down on their noses."

■ ■ ■

B Company was spread out so far that I spent most of my time travelling. There was always something going on, and I made it a habit to see any man from B Company who was in the hospital. The group at Exeter was having some trouble about which they needed to talk to the Company Commander. The Regimental Commander wanted all of his officers to report to Regimental Headquarters for a meeting. I spent so much time on the road that I had a hard time remembering what I was doing when I stopped at Tidworth. This rocked on until December 20. I kept on hearing rumors: B Company was coming back together and was to be moved. Well, well, sure enough, on December 22 we moved. We were going to Cheltenham to the big Service of Supply Headquarters. We were to be General John C. H. Lee's Security Company. Some people called him "Court House" Lee; we called him "Church House" Lee. Other people called him "Jesus Christ Himself," but General Lee was always good to B Company.

War changes things so fast that it is rather hard to keep up. General Lee was a Division Commander in 1940, and he had a Regimental Commander by the name of Colonel William G. Weaver. Over the years they must have developed considerable respect for each other's ability to do their jobs. At the end of 1940, when President Roosevelt sounded the alarm to bring many of the National Guard Divisions into active duty to teach them more about fighting, General Lee's job suddenly changed. He turned up again on a staff that was being put together for an overseas assignment. General Lee was appointed to the important job of G-4 for the European Theater of Operations. He went looking around for Officers to fill vacant spots in his command.

Colonel Weaver was just a little bit old to go overseas—he had graduated West Point in 1912. But there were so many people who knew him from the first World War, when he had commanded the 8th Machine Gun Battalion in the 3rd "Rock of the Marne" Division at Chateau Thierry, that there were a lot of people trying to get him assigned to their commands. General Middleton told me he wanted Weaver because he knew he could count on Weaver to fight. Colonel Weaver worked hard—his dedication to the Army and his ability and love to fight just couldn't be set aside when war was gathering. He was not the best man for sitting behind a desk; he loved the action that could only be found in the combat divisions. It pained Colonel Weaver to think that he might be left at home.

General Lee soon discovered that he had a job for Weaver overseas in England, but Weaver would have to be promoted to Brigadier General first. A number of the right people were contacted in Washington to get Congressional approval for Colonel Weaver to be promoted to General Weaver, and overseas he went.

General Weaver became Field Coordinator to Services of Supply, G-4, General Lee. It didn't take long before General Weaver was seated in a beautiful Packard. It was not a Cadillac, but with the pecking order being what it was, not a lot of Cadillacs were being handed out. General Weaver loved his car and saw to it that it was well taken care of, oil changed, well greased, gassed, washed, and waxed.

So, Field Coordinator General Weaver went travelling around England doing his job; he admitted that the Packard rode considerably better than a jeep. The General told me that he planned on riding down the main street in Berlin in his Packard just as soon as the shooting stopped. I thought this was fine.

I saw the Packard now and then in England by accident when it just happened to go by on the way somewhere. I was happy to have two jeeps assigned to my company. This I thought was great because I was like all infantry people: we loved the jeep. The little truck could take us just about anywhere a mule could go. It was about as tough as one, too. It saved a lot of soldiers from a lot of long, hard miles of walking, and infantry never suffers a shortage of walking.

We moved into a little one-company camp that needed a lot of cleaning up. We had been doing other jobs for so long that we were out of practice for the things we had been trained to do. It took a whole lot of time to get our timing back in marching and close order drill. We were issued some special equipment: four water-cooled machine guns, which we had to learn to shoot. These were our only defense against aircraft. We practiced with the guns, did more aircraft identification, and then went down on the coast to fire at a sleeve target being towed by a British airplane. We did very well; we didn't hit the airplane at all.

That was the only time we practiced with the guns, but we knew how, and we were ready.

Part of this detail was to make everything and everybody look sharp. We had to be ready for inspection every day. As usual, all the way to the garbage cans.

General Lee put out orders that there would be no waste of food. When you went through the mess lines at meal time you took all you wanted, and you ate it—and there was an officer or

Above: General William H. Weaver.

noncom at the Mess Hall door to see that there was nothing edible left on your tray. If there were food left over on the serving line, the Mess Sergeant had better have something good to make with leftovers. One day General Lee and some of his officers came over for inspection of his new Security Company B. Naturally he looked in the garbage can, where Mess Sergeant Landry had emptied a box of raisins. The General asked, "What are these raisins doing in the garbage can?"

Above: Homefront food production, England, April 1943. (FDR Library)

Mess Sergeant Landry said right away, "They're rancid, General," never expecting what happened next.

The General reached down into the garbage can, picked up some raisins, put them in his mouth, and started chewing. He said, "They don't taste rancid."

Sergeant Landry said, "I'll get them out of there right away, wash them, and have them served." And out they came.

The big concern in this food business was shipping space. If each man dumped one-third of a pound of food in the garbage each meal, by the end of each day he would have thrown away one pound of food. At the end of the month, that would be thirty pounds. Now you may notice this guy is not by himself in Cheltenham; there were maybe twenty thousand soldiers going to a mess hall somewhere every day. If all of them had eating habits like the first soldier, that would be about twenty thousand pounds of waste per day. At the end of the month, 20,000 pounds times 30 days is room on a boat for several tanks, trucks, or airplanes.

That's what General Lee, Commander of G-4 ETOUSA, was concerned about. General Lee was in charge of every bit of equipment and personnel that needed transportation from and to the Department of the Interior, that is, the United States.

Leftovers weren't the only waste we had to account for. Someone mentioned "Honeydew Buckets" within earshot, so I said, "What's a 'Honeydew Bucket'?"

So this guy says, "Sit down and I'll explain." Honeydew is a system by which human waste is collected and turned into fertilizer for the sake of the farmers who are growing crops. It starts off with something that looks like a 30-gallon bucket. The buckets are placed in the latrines under the holes. When a person goes to the latrine, he drops his load in the bucket, wipes himself, and throws the paper in a trash can. Then on an appointed day, the Honeydew picker-uppers come in, take the buckets, put clean buckets in place, and away they go. I don't know where they go, or how many places they pick up from. I only saw them putting this fertilizer into a field once. I hoped I hadn't been eating potatoes from that field!

After this explanation, little questions came to my mind. Would England get higher out of the sea for piling this fertilizer in the fields? Would England stay the same because the plants take different minerals out of the ground? We ate the plants, and the Honeydew system put the minerals back into the ground. I guess that would be equilibrium.

In field sanitation lectures there was always considerable discussion of such things. Like, for instance, one man will make one little pile a day. We taught a soldier to dig himself a little hole in the ground and do his disposable business in it and cover it up when he was finished. That one little pile in that one little hole wouldn't be too bad. Even if there were no hole, that one little pile still wouldn't be so bad, but with a hundred men, the pile would get larger and certainly disturbing! When the number rises to 20,000 little piles together, that would get to be a great big pile of feces. I guess that the Louisiana maneuvers, with five or six divisions (of maybe 20,000 each) running around in the boondocks and making their little holes, must have helped enrich the soil of Louisiana's Kisatchie Natural Forest very much. I'm glad I was never in the horse cavalry. They had a real problem with horse dung!

Above: Captain Mayhall at the Plough Hotel in Cheltenham. "We were drinking in the hotel bar, and I noticed a familiar looking man beside me. We had a little conversation. It was like running into a familiar face in the grocery store, someone you have been seeing day in and day out doing something ordinary like shopping, wondering who it is. You know the first second who it was you had met when his picture pops up in the newspaper, but you can't place him in a grocery store. I didn't realize it was Burgess Meredith I had been sitting with until I saw his next film."

So much for certain aspects of Army life. In our new camp we had room for the Mess Hall, 1st Sergeant and Company Clerk's Office and Company Commander's office, and another room large enough for the Supply Sergeant's room. There were three huts into each of which we managed to stuff a platoon of 40 men. There was one duty officer who spent the night at camp. The rest of the officers were quartered in the Plough Hotel on High Street, a hotel that the Americans took over for housing.

We were one company on detached service from Battalion and Regimental control, so we had to do our guard detail schedule and at the same time we had to have a training schedule that would help keep everyone alert and strong. We made our own training schedule and sent a copy to Battalion, Regiment, and the people we had to report to at the big headquarters at Ben Hall Farms.

Our new Headquarters wanted B Company to take part in some of their planned activities. We would join their troops for retreat on special days.

The first parade came on December 31, which was not long after our depot detail. But considering all things, B Company looked great. It got to be a fairly regular thing to have retreat, where all the units that had enough troops to march came to the large parade ground, listened to the orders of the day, and passed in review.

I got to be friends with the band director, and one night when we were having a beer or two I asked him if it would hurt anybody's feelings if he played "Dixie" when B Company was approaching the reviewing stand. Being as how he was from below the Mason-Dixon Line, he said he didn't think so. For the next five or six parades, when B Company approached the reviewing stand, the band struck "Dixie." B Company couldn't help but straighten their ranks and throw out their chests, and every foot came down in unison. When the command for "eyes right" came, every head snapped to the right, and we passed the reviewing stand and executed the "eyes front" with complete precision.

I didn't think anything of this, because back in the States during the regimental parades and division parades it was not unexpected to hear "Dixie" two or three times. But this was not so in the European Theater of Operations. The Adjutant began by saying that he really didn't mind Southern music, but he was against playing it too much, especially "Dixie."

I tried to explain to the Adjutant that our regiment, 156th Infantry, were members of the 31st Infantry Division, the "Dixie Division," and our bands played "Dixie" so much we really did not notice. I told the Adjutant that we liked all of John Philip

Sousa's marches, but that he would be missing some good music if "Dixie" was cut off the schedule. Pride in one's outfit makes a whole lot of difference. The Adjutant thought I might be trying to wake up a little bit of that Civil War sentiment. I didn't have this in mind. However, I did know that both the North and the South had soldiers that any Commander would be proud to command.

■   ■   ■

B Company worked hard at our job as Security Company General Lee's G-4 ETOUSA Headquarters. B Company also worked very hard·to keep fit. For, as we had already found out, we never knew what they might decide to use us for next. We had run a G-4 depot, an overflow depot, motor pool, and now we were providing security for a large headquarters. This headquarters was responsible for everything that moved. The first question was where the storage area would be located for thousands of trucks, tanks, airplanes, many different kinds of boats, and training grounds for troops. This was only in the planning stage, and had to be coordinated with the British. British landowners were brought into the planning, for many civilians had to house both British and American troops, to say nothing of changing some of their land into shooting ranges.

When the African operation began, England was stripped of combat troops. The 29th Division (Infantry) and the 156th Infantry Regiment were all the troops left in England. If the Germans had guessed this, I suppose they would not have put so much of their fighting forces in Russia.

For us this was a planning and building year. Troops were being trained in the United States, and there were combat divisions being blooded in Africa. Some of them would come back to England when the African campaign was over, to say nothing of the British troops that would come home for R&R, refitting, and replacements. New equipment was being developed—larger, faster tanks and better long-range airplanes. One other thing was needed: larger and faster ships to transport this better

Above: 37mm antitank gun still in use at Camp Carson training camp in Colorado, 1943. (FDR Library)

equipment and all these troops being trained in the United States and Canada. German submarines were giving hell to the shipments. The Germans were sinking our ships right at the mouth of the Mississippi River. Some of my company, including Mess Sergeant Landry, lived in Morgan City, close to the Gulf of Mexico. They were not seeing any fighting in England. They thought they could do more at home.

One of the most important operations for the Americans was our experience in Africa. At the beginning, the American light tanks were equipped with 37mm antitank guns. A 37mm projectile against a German tank was like throwing tennis balls against the side of a city bus. The 37mm was good maybe to damage the treads on a tank, shoot holes in trucks and passenger cars, and scare the hell out of an individual soldier. Against tanks, it might at best wake up the German gunner behind his 88mm.

The regimental anti-tank companies were equipped with 37mm so-called antitank guns in 1942. I am sure these guns were replaced in Africa. Larger tanks with greater firepower were developed and brought into combat. I sometimes wonder what our military was doing before the war that they didn't see what type of tanks the German engineers were putting in the field. There were people like General Patton, whose life's work was admiring tanks, designing uniforms and helmets for tankers, devising the best track design and engine power to say nothing of gun design. There probably were many good men whose good ideas and designs on paper for better fighting equipment were not noticed until Pearl Harbor. From Pearl Harbor on, anything that sounded better than what we already had, Congress would throw money at it.

In the 156th Infantry Regiment we began to notice the changes. In 1941 we were wearing out World War I's wrapped wool leggings and wool riding britches in summertime. These were replaced with canvas lace-up leggings. We had all qualified with the Springfield 1903 rifle; this was replaced by the eight-shot M1 Garand, so we had to qualify again—which made us better shots. In place of our hats, our beautiful hats that made us look like the "Rough Riders" on foot, they offered us some nice overseas caps and helmets that we wore until the end of the war. We traded our campaign hats for helmets. Considering the amount of shrapnel that dented them and bounced off, we became good friends with our helmets.

1943 brought more peculiar-looking people in uniform to the big G-4 Headquarters at Cheltenham. "Peculiar looking" because they were not soldiers—never had been—but they were the very best in their fields. Doctors had come to headquarters to get their orders as to what part of the medical units they would join. People from the best cooking and bakery centers were here to figure out the easiest and most convenient package for the individual soldier. We called them K rations. K rations were designed to be eaten under combat conditions. The little box usually contained a can of food of some kind, a biscuit to gnaw on, a small pack of cigarettes, powdered coffee, and some-thing sweet. The boxes were covered with wax so that they would burn with very little smoke. We held our canteen cups over these little burning boxes, and *voilà*! Hot coffee!

The best men in communications, best in transportation, or any expert in any field that the Army needed were there. They were able to communicate their ideas to those people in businesses back in the United States who could put their ideas in motion. Better foods, better delivery, and no shortages. Better airplanes with better fuel. The 100-octane fuels that gave our fighter planes more power than the Luftwaffe were developed at a Baton Rouge refinery.

1943 was also a big year for build-up of the air war. The British had been fighting the air war by themselves for some time, and they were doing a good job with their night bombing raids on France and Germany, but manpower was getting to be a problem. It was a big boost to be joined by Canadians, Australians, and Americans easing across the Canadian border to get in on the excitement, and Polish, French, and Scandinavians who slipped out of their countries to join in the battle against the Nazi war machine. Many of these non-British turned up sitting behind the controls of fighters and bombers in the Royal Air Force.

Britain's ability to build enough fighters and bombers was in question. British industry of all kinds had taken a heavy beating. People had to be retrained, and new means of transportation for supply and distribution of these rebuilt industries had to be found. Problems arose with supplies, shops to work in, people to do the job. The Germans had bombed so much of British industry that new places, hidden places, remote places had to be constructed to put out spare parts for new planes.

America turned its great industrial strength into the building of airplanes, tanks, trucks, ships, and all their allied parts. In addition, the United States came to the aid of the British with fighting ships, raw materials, planes, tanks—to say nothing of gasoline, oil, and even food. The Russians were also allies, and the first year the Germans pushed the Russians back and destroyed so much of their fighting equipment that the Americans had to work out a way to support the Russians any way they could. For a while the Germans had the Russians down on their knees. Germany badly needed to capture their oil fields.

*Above: WAAF balloon operators in England report for inspection before
going off duty after a strenuous day of training on the balloon site.
(National Archives, NWDNS-306-NT-1285F(3))*

The Russians didn't just sit and wait for help. They boxed up
a lot of their war industries and hauled them to the east of
Moscow. There, shops were set up to rebuild fighting equipment
that the Germans thought they had completely destroyed.
Stalin was very interested in getting the English and Ameri-
cans to start fighting on the ground in Europe to get some of the
German war machine off the Russians' backs. The Battle of
Stalingrad had killed millions of men.

We were not only planning, building, training; we were also
learning. It was rather quiet in England except for the air war.
The British were bombing Germany at night, and the Ameri-

cans were bombing with hundreds of planes every day. We were fighting in North Africa, and when that closed out, the Americans and British took Sicily by amphibious landings and then went into the south of Italy. This was good because we learned what kind of equipment we needed to make this sort of landing. Considering the Japanese war and the disaster in France, we needed better than we had. Landing in Italy helped the Russians a little bit, because it held many German troops in Italy and kept them from joining the assault on Russia.

The United States, with its need of military personnel, soon recognized that it had a great unused labor pool. America had a population of ladies who had been used to sell clothes, take dictation, type letters. It was quickly noted that these ladies could use a rivet gun to put airplanes together, could weld ships, fly airplanes from factories to ports of embarkation, drive trucks, run tractors in the fields. The ladies had gone into oil refineries and learned to do electrical work as well as mechanical work and laboratory work, every aspect of the oil business.

When the time came, many joined the women's corps of the Army, Navy, and Air Corps; many were used to release men from office work. They sold war bonds, they ran canteens for the soldiers, and they visited the hospitals where the newly wounded soldiers were being brought. In England the ladies worked in what they called the Land Army. They worked in factories, let balloons up and down on cables during air raids to confuse German pilots as to how low they could fly, drove trucks and ambulances, served as nurses, and worked as radio operators plotting boards for the Navy and the Royal Air Force. It seemed to me these ladies were happy to be part of the war effort and to do something while they waited for their husbands and boyfriends to come back. For some this was the best money they ever made.

■ ■ ■

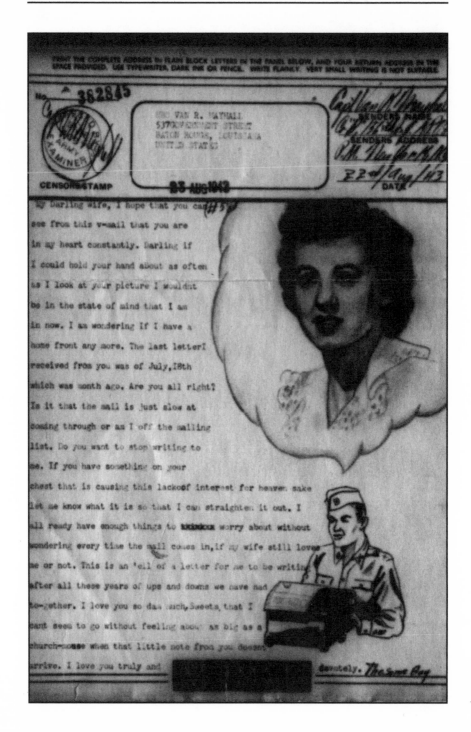

Maggie's Drawers

I began to notice that the training schedule of Company B was looking a whole lot the same from week to week, so I thought I had better work up some new ideas. I put in for some British schools right away and managed to get accepted to the London District School of Battle Drill. It was a thirty-day school starting July 20 for four weeks at Christ Church in southern England. I went to this school overweight, but when I came back I had lost thirty pounds. I learned a lot, too. The British had been in this fighting business so long that they knew a lot that I needed to learn. I had a hard time understanding the way the British explained problems, so I didn't always know what was going on—I had heard over the years that the two English speaking-countries were "divided by a common language," and now I saw it for myself.

I was billeted with the only other captain on the course, Michael Ramsey, British. We met in our room. I jumped to shake hands, and we had very few words, and I sat down on my cot and looked the Captain over. He was what I thought was typical English—tall, chest sort of sunken in, didn't look like he had been out in the sun in a very long time. I didn't see how he could make this course, because I had heard it was rough. It was.

The next morning we were on parade in battle dress, and the head instructor said, "We have fifteen minutes before class, let's run a mile." Off we went; full of breakfast, we did our mile. I managed to run our mile and sit through the class, and then I asked to be excused for a minute or two. I went to the latrine and upchucked every thing I had eaten for a week.

When I came back, the instructor was waiting for me. He said, "I say, Yank, did you get in shape for this course?"

I replied, "No, sir."

He said, "It's going to be bloody rough," and then, "Are you ready to go?"

I said, "Yes," and off we went. For the next three days, it was running, climbing, jumping, crawling, sliding, and wishing I was in condition. My "striker" woke me up in the mornings and poured a canteen cup of tea down me, and by Thursday of the first week I was beginning to breathe again. I had quit smoking. I couldn't handle a cigarette.

Thursday was my turn to carry the Bren gun, the automatic that the British squad was equipped with. It was heavy, and it was the first time I ever had the thought, "If I could only fall down and break my leg so I could quit!" But I was the senior American on the course, and there were only six Americans altogether, so I couldn't even groan. I had to go on.

Christ Church had everything that was needed for a good battle school. Areas of towns close by had been bombed by the Germans, and there was room to practice street fighting, breaking down doors, blowing holes in walls, and throwing live grenades through windows. There were valleys that were better-than-average obstacle courses. So we went through these on the way to where we were going for practice.

One day we were going to be exposed to live fire. We had to determine how many people were opposing us—a squad, two squads, a platoon. We, the student platoon, were sitting in a slit trench. I looked to the direction from which the live fire would come, and saw some bushes that looked like they could deflect a bullet. I moved over and sat down. The show started with a half-squad firing, and we got the idea that lower might be better. The whole squad began to fire. This was the first time that I had heard the muzzle blast from .30-caliber rifles.

A second squad opened fire, and I was sure lower was better, and all of a sudden I heard a loud yell not far from me. One of the students had moved in and sat right in the spot that I had moved from. He had been sitting with his knees up and his hands locked around his knees, and one of those .30-caliber slugs ricocheted off a limb and went right through the bottom of his left forearm. This wound didn't count for a Purple Heart.

The British could be singleminded about what they were doing, so they took the wounded student out and back to shooting we went. I know that I was supposed to pick up on what size group was shooting at us, so we could decide what to do—attack or dig deeper. However, I was distracted by those flying bullets and only learned to keep my head down.

This school was made up of two platoons; one platoon of officers and the other platoon of noncoms. Both platoons were there for the same thing: to introduce the students to more and better ways of confounding the enemy forces. The noncoms were competing against the officer platoon. I don't think they quite knew what to do with American noncoms, so they were put in the officer platoon. As the school settled down to working out the problems given to us during the night, particularly where the two platoons had to maneuver against each other, the competition got more aggressive. The noncoms took great pleasure in making the officers look like they had left most of their marbles at home. After some of the night problems, as we appeared on parade in the mornings, there were black eyes on both the officer platoon and the noncom platoon.

The officer platoon was assigned the problem of going out and picking up a prisoner. We were given the general area where the German line (the noncoms) was located. Off we sneaked into the dark, creeping and crawling, and before long our platoon had come up with a prisoner. The prisoner didn't like his situation; so, at what he thought was a good time, he took off running in the dark and the high grass.

One of our platoon, Sergeant Little, a tall, blondish, freckled American, said, "I'll get him!"

In the dark we could hear the running of two people, then a noise like two men rolling around in the dry weeds in frantic competition. Suddenly there was a noise that sounded like someone had slapped a side of beef with a meat cleaver. Everything got quiet for a moment, and then out of the dark came a voice that said, "I got him."

On our last big problem of the course, we were given information on a need-to-know basis. The first need-to-know was, "Load on to the lorries and proceed to a port of embarkation to be assigned boats." At midnight we loaded on some kind of fast assault boat and took off. I wondered where we were going. At the rate we were travelling we could have landed in France. We went buzzing down around close to the Isle of Wight and then into the southern shore of England, where we were given a slip of paper with instructions. "Be at R.V.—"

I figured that was British for *where we meet*; it turned out it was short for "rendezvous"—

"—at daylight fifteen miles inland. There is an aerodrome guarded by dogs that has to be avoided. There are troops that will be looking for you.

"Do not be captured."

We were supposed to be British Commandos in a German-occupied country. Our mission was to get into a German tank park, destroy the tanks, and get out.

We slipped off the assault boats and started inland. We were travelling as fast as we could in the dark, so I guess we were not as quiet as we should have been. About five minutes inland, we came to a road with thick hedges on both sides. We started crossing the road, and a group of troops started after us from the right and then a group from the left. We looked for a place to dive through the hedge but the troops fell all over us. One of them had a big stick over his shoulder and started pounding us with it.

They had me spread-eagled in the road, and this guy was waving that stick in my face. He says, "Hey, Yank, you give up?"

I said, "Can you think of anything else I can do?"

They laughed and tied us up so we couldn't run off. But they got careless and started looking for more of us, and we took off again. We were more careful, but we covered a lot of ground fast, and we arrived at the R.V. just as daylight began to show. We put out guards, and those who could began cooking on low fires, and we spent the day quiet and doing reconnaissance to find the tank park.

The tank park was about seven miles from where we were camped. Just as soon as the moon came up, we took off on com-

Above: London District School class photo, with nicknames.

pass, easing through the British bogs (a lot like Mississippi wet muds). We finally arrived on the edge of the tank park and had a great time running in and out throwing firecrackers all over everywhere. When we had done enough damage, we had to get the hell out of there. Our mission was not to fight, but to get in, destroy, and get out. The opposing troops began to fire on us, so off we went. This ended the problem, and we could then be picked up and returned to the billet. We all cleaned up for a lecture from the Colonel. He seemed pleased with us in general and wished us well, and I said good-bye to Battle School.

I was delighted to get back to B Company. B Company was still on detached service from our Battalion and from our Regiment, and they seemed to think that we were getting along well enough without any help from them. I started using some of what I learned at school right away. The British had learned to do a lot of things in a small space and taught us to do the same. I took stock of the space we had and laid out an obstacle course, monkey rack, and an area that we used at night for trip-wire obstacle courses. We used the Cotswold Hills for marches. In one place stone had been cut out of the side of one of the hills. We used this quarry for mountain climbing.

Above, left: Looking trim, Capt. Mayhall takes a break at the Ambassador hotel in Bournemouth after attending Battle School; right: Van Mayhall and Dick Goodwin, reconnaissance pilot. Below, left: With two other officers at the Ambassador; right: Three officers pose in a window on "High Street" of B Company's post.

The officers of B Company took a beating in some of these training activities. My executive officer, Lieutenant Champagne, broke his leg on the obstacle course; and while I was climbing up the wall in the stone quarry, I reached up and caught an outcropping that was sandstone, and it gave way. I bounced from hedge to hedge until I landed at the bottom in a growth of English nettle—the stinging kind. The fall didn't hurt me, but that English nettle put little holes I didn't need in a lot of places.

The first time General Weaver visited our company, he found me near the monkey rack and obstacle course. His jeep pulled up, and he stepped out with another officer, a Major. The General asked me what the equipment was for, and I explained that I had built the course to keep my men in shape.

General Weaver said to the Major, "Can you do that course?"

The Major shook his head. "I don't think so, sir," he said.

General Weaver turned to me and said, "Show me how it's done." I climbed through the monkey rack, climbed along the ropes, and came out the other side. The General thanked me and went on his way. General Weaver came back to inspect the company many times after that, observing training exercises and our Company's overall appearance.

The Company worked out more night problems. We blackened our faces, made sure we had no jingling equipment, and started slipping into areas that were guarded. Most of the people on guard did not have ammunition, which was all right with us. We needed the practice, but we didn't need to get shot at.

We were beginning to feel that we needed some weapons practice. Our last visit to the firing ranges had been back in Camp Bowie. The only kind of ammunition we had was the .50 caliber that we had for the machine guns that we were manning as part of our security company mission. We had hardly enough .45 ammo to keep a clip full for the Officer of the Day, the Sergeant of the Guard, and the Corporal of the Guard. No .30 caliber, no 60mm mortar. So we decided to do something about it. We knew that there were all kinds of ammunition at the 156th Infantry Headquarters.

Part of A Company (my former company) was manning the ammunition depot, and so Sergeant Robichaux and I hooked our jeep trailer up, and away we went. It was so nice to have friends in the right places.

We drove the sixty-five miles and turned into the ammunition depot and stopped at the shack. I went in, and there was my old friend Lieutenant Edgar Chaney as Ammunition Officer of the Day. "Mayhall, come in and have some coffee."

Before I went in to visit with Lieutenant Chaney, I told my 1st Sergeant to look around and see what could be found.

Lieutenant Chaney brought me up to date on what was going on at the regiment and how the Combat Landing School was doing. He told me it was because of the school that his ammunition dump was loaded with all the ammo they needed and some extra. After a long time, my Sergeant showed up and suggested that we get on the road. I said, "I'd like to finish my coffee."

Sergeant Robichaux said, "I think it's time to leave right now, sir." So I thanked Lieutenant Chaney for the coffee, and we took off.

I asked Sergeant Robichaux what the hurry was, and he said: "I don't think that we would like to have this trailer inspected."

I said, "You all met some friends out in the ammo dump?"

He said, "Captain, they were very generous; everything we wanted and more. We have seven-hundred-sixty rounds of 60mm mortar, boxes of .30 caliber, .45 caliber, some dynamite, and all kinds of other explosives, with those push-pull booby traps that we need to learn about."

We didn't have any place to put all this, so we stored it in the supply room, where the supply sergeant slept. He didn't sleep very well.

Just as soon as we could, we went looking for mortar ranges, rifle ranges, pistol ranges, and ranges we could use to fire machine guns. The British had closed these ranges, but permission was given for us to use them. We put the mortar section on the training schedule right away. We had them dry-shooting in the company area before we put them on the range. It had been so long since they had fired the mortars that I didn't want any accidents. By the time we fired all of that 60mm mortar ammunition, the mortar section crews were able to drop rounds in a five-foot square from 500 yards.

We went through our dry shooting of the .30 caliber and then we went to the ranges. One of the familiar shouts heard when new recruits are on the firing range is "Maggie's Drawers," then the men in the pits wave a flag at the shooter. "Maggie's Drawers" is an undergarment-shaped flag, waved at the shooter when the whole target is missed. Well, it was a lot better with seasoned troops: We did some shooting at still targets, and then we went to the combat ranges where targets pop up with the sound of a firecracker. The shooter has to get the target quickly, from the hip or shoulder.

Shooting with the .45 automatic pistol is not a real sure thing: The closer to a target the shooter is, the greater the chances of hitting something. The .45 has great stopping power, but its recoil is powerful and not easy to get used to. It takes lots of training and practice to become a good shot.

In the meantime, General Lee was making plans and thinking about the last time that his drivers had had training of any kind. A General's driver is supposed to do a lot more than drive. The drivers are part of the General's security—fight, shoot, and drive. General Lee had visited B Company at different times and saw some of the training that we went through. So, one day I got orders to put six of the General's drivers through a toughen-up course for a while. Fortunately, the drivers who came over were tickled to have a change of pace. We were not going to have time for field inspections, twenty-mile marches, and night problems. We did have time for individual combat, knife fighting, and weapons use.

The drivers had not been selected because they were nice boys. They were tough and they just needed a little working out with people who were strong, fast, and good with infantry weapons. Each one arrived with a Tommy gun and a .45. We skipped the rifle ranges and went to combat ranges where they could fire their Tommy guns at quick-appearing targets. Fortunately, they knew their Tommy guns better than we did, so we learned a little from them. We kept them two weeks longer than we were supposed to. When we released them, they seemed to have enjoyed the experience. They stood a little straighter, moved a little quicker, and they all came by to say "Thanks."

■ ■ ■

August and September whisked by, and October went just as fast. In Battle School, we did a little practicing getting on and off moving trucks. So we borrowed a 1½-ton truck and B Company started practicing coming from cover (hiding along the road) and grabbing and jumping onto the bed of the truck. When we got off the still-moving truck, it was "come down backward running and get into cover right away." It worked pretty well; we didn't break any legs nor did we ruin any equipment. Needless to say, this operation is not done at high speed but at a trotting speed.

We watched the build-up of G-4 Headquarters, which was getting more and more crowded. New sections of this big Supply Headquarters were popping up all over the place. The crowding got serious when my officers and I were billeted in the home of an old British Colonel. We had a big room and a little bitty fireplace, and it had turned winter, and it was cold. Lieutenant Champagne and I brought a roll of medical tape to put over some of the cracks to slow the wind down as it blew through the room. We spent sleeping time there only. We must have bathed at the Company because I can't remember taking a bath or shower in that cold house.

We were located close to a field called Gloucester Air-Craft. I didn't know all of what they did or manufactured there; the British were clever at hiding what they were doing on the ground because the Germans were doing their best to find out from the air. For example: Also close to B Company camp was a schoolhouse. Every now and then I would see people playing soccer on the schoolground, but never any children. One day I had occasion to go into the building. I was let in, not very far, but far enough to see men working at machinery that was spitting out aircraft parts as fast as it could. I knew they must have been transporting these new parts out to where planes were being repaired or built. I knew they must have been transporting raw material in. But I never saw any trucks.

It is nice to think that one is in on something new early—that is, before it is smeared all over the papers. From our company location, we had been seeing a different type of airplane flying around. One day I saw this odd-looking plane making passes at a low British fighter plane. Smoke was coming out of the two motors that hung under each wing, and the tail was higher than that on other planes.

I thought the plane should be put in the shop and a ring job done on the motors. A few days later the wind changed, and this odd-looking plane had to land from our end of the runway and came fairly low over our camp. A group of us were watching it, and I looked and said, "That thing doesn't have any propellers on it." I remembered that I had read somewhere that the Italians had developed a jet airplane that would go about 125 miles an hour. I was amazed the British had developed an aircraft that would "fly like a bat out of hell" and I was one of the first Americans to see it. I had been in England over a year, so if the United States was experimenting with jets, I had no way of knowing.

I was aware that the United States was building an awful lot of B-17 bombers and a lot of fighters—P-47s (Thunderbolts) and P-51s (Mustangs). *Stars and Stripes* would publish every now and then how many B-17s were shot down. On one daylight bombing raid into Germany fifty bombers were shot down. Put into "infantry language" that turned out to be five hundred men killed in action, missing in action, or taken prisoner. This loss was before long-range fighters were there to accompany the bombers to their targets. I always thought that bombing was dangerous work, sitting in my foxhole looking up into the clear blue and watching the B-17s and B-25s heading into Germany, the German 88mm and 105mm anti-aircraft guns firing away with large puffs of black smoke dotting the sky all around the flight path of the bombers. This made me feel a little more comfortable right there in my foxhole.

I do not know when the P-51 Mustang fighter aircraft came onto the war scene, but a group of British pilots arrived at the Greenville Air Force Base in Mississippi to learn how to fly this hot fighter in late 1942 or early 1943. My cousin Elizabeth Ann Mayhall, daughter of my Uncle Not, lived in Greenville then. Elizabeth met one of the pilots, Richard Goodwin, and soon they were married. Dick was sent back to England to join the air war, and Elizabeth caught a tramp steamer carrying war materials to England.

When Elizabeth turned up in London, there was much telephone conversation between Greenville and Baton Rouge to find out where I was. I had not seen or talked to Elizabeth since we were sixteen years old. When a letter arrived giving me her address, I immediately gathered together a few little things like sugar and rice that I knew were hard to get if you were a civilian, and off I went to London. After so many dead ends and turn arounds, I finally found the Goodwin home where Elizabeth was staying with her in-laws. I don't think Mrs. Goodwin ever believed that I was who I said I was. I think she had heard too many stories about those wild Americans who chased Indians and shot buffalo.

In the meantime, Flight Officer Dick Goodwin had been placed in a reconnaissance squadron. He would fly over the previous night's bomber raids and take pictures of the targets that were supposed to have been destroyed. One thing about the reconnaissance planes is that they put so much camera equipment and gasoline in them it would make them too heavy to put a few machine guns on for protection. When a German fighter gets after you and your recon plane, you are supposed to "cock her back" and head for home.

Dick, in addition to flying reconnaissance in P-51s, flew British planes. The British took time out to train him to fly a plane called the "Mosquito." The Mosquito was a two-motored, fast plane that could fly on one motor and was made of glued-together plywood—a good plane for reconnaissance deep into Germany. It could carry lots of camera equipment and 100-octane gasoline.

■   ■   ■

Above: The "Infantry Mite." "B Company got kind of fed up with the air force in England talking about their 'Gremlins,' so we worked up the Infantry Mite. This little bug bedevilled all infantrymen. He threw dust into weapons just before inspection. He had a stinger. He held a soldier's booted foot in the mud. He wore hobnailed shoes and walked all over your skin so you couldn't stop itching. He would hold up the mail. He was cocky, mischievous, very insulting, and caused all the problems in the 'Gaw-dammed' Infantry. An artist in the company, Sgt. Joseph Arseneaux, drew pictures for all our letters.

"The Infantry Mite was B Company's alone. There were pictures of him hanging in our day room pitching softball and riding a soldier's pack, making it heavier as the miles went on. He was suspected of having something to do with Lt. Roland Champagne breaking a leg on our obstacle course."

Tea with the King

I took stock of B Company and General Lee's Headquarters. This guard duty that we were to perform was not the grubby, crawl-in-the-mud sort of thing that we had been used to. It was a spit-and-polish, heel-clicking, quick-salute and double "sir" job. Well, we cleaned, polished, shaved, shined and sharpened our movements in all ways to get the job done. We still remembered we were infantry; we exercised, marched, trained in rifle, bayonet, map work, and individual combat.

Well, they liked us. They inspected us, they commended us, they were glad to have us around.

I was called in one day by the Headquarters Commandant and was told that I was being sent to London. I asked, "Is my Company going also?" The colonel explained that I had been selected to attend a tea at Buckingham Palace for junior officers. No Company. The colonel told me I would get orders and an invitation shortly.

Sure enough, in a few days there were my orders and my invitation to the tea party. *Why me?* I thought, then, *How me?* Little ole boy grew up six blocks from Third Street, went to school in Catfish Town and not that good of a student, and here I am fixing to go to a party with England's finest.

I went to London on a Saturday and reported to the billeting office for a place to spend the night. When I gave them my name, they told me they knew who I was and why I was in London. The billeting officer said, "Capt. Mayhall, we have a room for you in the Cumberland Hotel, and would you like to go to the show tonight?" Well, it turned out that Irving Berlin was in London for the premiere of the great wartime show that he wrote and directed, *This is the Army,* and I was invited to see it, too.

They put me in the rows that they saved for the press, the first and second rows down front. I was nearly on stage. It was wonderful; it meant so much to me. Needless to say, I enjoyed it.

Sunday morning, November 24, came around fast enough. I polished boots and buttons, got my tie and shirt looking the best possible. If you are going to the palace you have to look your finest, even when you're sure nobody is going to give you a second look. At 3:15 P.M. I arrived at Buckingham Palace and was told, "Move to the Green Room."

There stood Mrs. Mayhall's youngest son in the Green Room of Buckingham Palace. All around me were many young officers like myself trying to maintain an even countenance, trying not to become giddy, trying to drink in the splendor. There were WACs and nurses there as well. This was storybook land. If there was anyone there that I knew, I didn't find him. We all shifted around looking up and down and wondering what was next.

Double doors to the Rose Room were opened by a uniformed servant. We were lined up and the presentations started. Just inside the Rose Room stood two more uniformed servants; the first was one of the assistants to the Master of the House. The second was the most important servant in the palace, the mighty, high-ranking Master of the House. As we entered the Rose Room single file, we handed our invitations to the first servant and he handed them to the Master of the House, who called out our names for all to hear.

After the Master of the House stood the King, who shook hands with each of us. Next to him stood the Queen, who also greeted us. Princess Elizabeth greeted us next. She was only a little girl, maybe ten or eleven years old. Finally we met the younger of the princesses, Margaret.

We then moved into a great hall where there were tables laden with snacks. Anything that you could think of (except Louisiana shrimp and crawfish!) was there to be tasted. The

King's scotch was excellent; I was no great judge, but it went down very well.

The King and Queen and the two little princesses mingled freely with us young soldiers. So, I talked to them freely. I asked them if they liked the Americans running all over hill and dale. The King told me that they had been needing some help and were glad we were here.

I knew that I would never have this opportunity again, so I wanted to make myself ask each one of them something, but all I could think to ask was the same thing, how did they like having the Americans there; the answers were all about the same. After that I went doodling and sampling around the tables snacking and doing a little bit of glass tipping and meeting some of the other guests.

I glanced up from a cracker-and-cheese dish and standing beside me was a young officer wearing a Silver Star. This was before the invasion, so not too many people had ribbons that are usually earned in ground force action. I told him I had always wanted to shake the hand of a guy who had earned the Silver Star. We shook hands and I gave my name and he mumbled a name that I did not catch. My eyes drifted down to his name tag, and it jumped out at me: *Roosevelt.*

I had a weekend that would be hard to top. I had seen *This is the Army* from the front row. I had met Irving Berlin. The play left me with music that still goes round and round in my head. The guy with the Silver Star was one of General Teddy Roosevelt's sons, grandson of Teddy Roosevelt. It wasn't news that Capt. Mayhall attended the party, but it was news to *Stars and Stripes* that Capt. Quentin Roosevelt attended.

I still have the invitation.

■ ■ ■

Air Raid

*C*hristmas was coming and I had written to Marie and asked if she could scare up some candy of any kind—we could use it. Our camp was about two blocks from an elementary school, and many of these kids hadn't seen candy in a long time. Marie went to work and managed to send about thirty-five pounds of hard candy. We made contact with the principal, and she was very excited about our offer to have a Christmas party at our camp. I think the teachers were rather happy to take a look at the wild Americans. They might even see an Indian! We never produced an Indian, but we produced plenty of good food, cake, and candy. Our one failure was the "ice cream" our cooks came up with. It was a near–ice cream, but we never were able to get it cold enough to be spooned. Lots of the kids liked it in liquid form. I have often wondered how many of those little people missed school the next day because of overeating. The teachers did let us know that everyone enjoyed themselves.

■ ■ ■

Throughout the winter a number of high-ranking officers came to look at us. I think they just wanted to see a unit that was made up of squads and platoons who drilled, marched, and worked together the way an infantry company was supposed to do. Our record day was seven generals; the highest rank among those generals was three star. We stayed on schedules that would keep us as close to being "fit for field duty" as possible.

I started a regular meeting of all noncoms and the Captain Company Commander. We would meet in the day room, and I would take off my captain's bars and put them on the table. I would start the questions by asking the group, "Any gripes, anything bad going on, anything good going on?"

The first gripe started with, "Those eggs we had for breakfast were terrible." Mess Sergeant Landry was right there, and I asked him if he had anything to say about the eggs. He told us they had been sitting out and were a little stale, and the next shipment would be better. His answer satisfied everybody (until the next shipment).

"When are we going to get off this security job?" I was the one who had to answer ones like that, and my answer usually was, "I have no idea."

One came from Sergeant Keller, who said, "We have a chance to take it easy for a while. Why don't we?"

I mulled this over long enough for the group to get quiet again, then I gave my answer. "We are in a shooting war right now. We don't know what will happen to us. I don't know that we will get into combat as a company. I don't know how many of us will get into combat, but I am sure that some of us will get into the shooting. Even if only one of us gets in the shooting war, I hope we will save his life by keeping up with our training."

As soon as D-Day arrived anyone who ever carried a rifle would be moved from England to France—and that is what happened to B Company, 156th Infantry, and the whole regiment. I was the first one to go.

■ ■ ■

You never know how things will work out and who it will work out for. We kept up our training and our exercises. Notification arrived that I was to report for another school. England was scraping the bottom of the barrel on personnel, so they designed a school to create instructors to pull up some of the people who had been turned down as unfit physically. B Company was not exactly in the sort of shape that needed to be built up very much, but I had asked for schools and this was one I could go to. I had decided after Battle School that if I could I would bring some of my noncoms along, just to let them know that the British were far from being soft.

On February 10, Staff Sergeant Michel, Staff Sergeant Davidson, and I left Cheltenham and headed for the London College of Physical Training. We would be there for two weeks. We were surprised at how much they managed to stuff into those two weeks. We started off double-timing and running, being taught to climb ropes, and how to get from the bottom side of a horizontal rope to the top side and slide across a river, and to climb up and down rope ladders, the kind one sees hanging off the side of ships. We had to swim, learn to tumble, and the worst was timed race-walking. We had to do a two-mile race walk in seventeen minutes. It doesn't sound bad—we only had rifle, helmet, light pack, shorts, shirt, and shoes. The first time we did this little conditioning exercise a big MP Sergeant passed out. When I heard his rifle hit the blacktop and his helmet go banging to the side of the street, I was surprised and embarrassed at the same time. I was embarrassed because I just didn't think Americans should fail a test at a British school. I was surprised because this MP Sergeant looked like he could have played football most anywhere.

That night I got my next surprise. The air-raid sirens went off and, with some of the British officers, we ran up to the roof to see what we could see. The 90mm, air defense, 40mm Bofors, 20mm cannons, and .50 machine guns were all firing up into the night sky. If you have ever been to a night football game and watched the cigarettes being lighted across the stadium, you can get some idea of the sight of exploding shells being fired at the German planes over London. The large spotlights were swinging back and forth looking for whatever the Germans had sent over. One plane was caught in a spotlight, and fire was concentrated on it. Whether he was shot down or not, I don't know.

About that time we began to hear this *plunk, plunk, plunk* noise. In the dark we couldn't see anything, and I asked the British officer standing next to me, "What's the noise?"

Above: A London street in ruins after an air raid. (FDR Library)

He said, "Yank, that's all that shrapnel coming back to the ground, and you might think about putting on your helmet." I thought this over about two seconds and headed for cover and my helmet.

This was my first full-blown air raid, and I felt elated to be on the 50-yard line where I could watch the action: the full rumble of all of our antiaircraft guns, British and American, in the protection of London. I saw the burst of shells seeking our enemy in the sky, and I felt that nothing could get through the terrible blanket of fire and metal that our side was throwing upward. I did begin to realize for the first time that all that metal we were throwing up had to come down somewhere, when it began to *thunk, thunk* all around where I was standing. This friendly fire was not so friendly coming down. I often wondered how many people in London were killed or wounded from all that metal. The next day we picked up pieces of shrapnel lying around with jagged edges from being torn apart by explosion.

Sergeants Michel and Davidson enjoyed the air raid and learned the difference between friendly fire, which went up, and the unfriendly fire aimed down. They did not enjoy the food as much as back with B Company because the English have a way of boiling and forgetting to use salt, pepper, and whatever else South Louisiana cooks use.

Our last day at school was taken up with a two-hour, ten-mile race walk at double time. We had to shoot as soon as we finished to see if we could fight after a forced march. My two sergeants and myself came in at full gallop in an hour and fifty-four minutes, and we did very well with our shooting. The British were impressed, and we went back to our unit with good evaluations on our papers. We all had more respect for the British. One or two of our instructors had been at Dunkirk. If you were alive after Dunkirk, you must have done a few things right.

Just as soon as Sergeant Michel, Sergeant Davidson, and I returned to B Company in Cheltenham, I set up a schedule for the noncoms of Company B. Each morning we (Company Commander and all noncoms) would meet in the mess hall that had been cleared of tables and chairs, and do a half hour of strength exercises that I had been introduced to at the physical training school. We used a follow-the-leader method of exercising. There was no count. Everyone moved in time with the leader of his group. As the physical training periods increased, the eyes of the noncoms became quicker and more alert, and it was hard for the leader to get them out of cadence. I was surprised that this eye coordination could work and become as proficient as it did.

When the noncoms had finished their daily workout with the Company Commander, they would then assemble their squads and platoons and go through the next morning workout. As time went by, I could see the change in strength and agility right down to the last man. When that last man goes from no pull-ups to twenty pull-ups and goes from ten push-ups to fifty push-ups, he gets pretty sure he can hold his own with the rest of his squad and platoon, and his pride and confidence make the whole Company a little more sure of itself.

■ ■ ■

Opposite: A heartfelt message home talks about the future, after the war.

Unfunny Stuff

*L*ate one night in March a Provost Marshal called me from Taunton and said, "Captain, I have one of your sergeants and one of your privates in jail. They are charged with assault and robbery."

I replied: "Lieutenant, that must be some kind of mistake." These two men had been with me for nearly two years, and I had never had any kind of trouble with them. It was about two o'clock in the morning, so I told the Lieutenant that I would be there by daylight. I made arrangements with my Executive Officer and notified 1st Sergeant Robichaux that he and I were going to Taunton.

When we got there, I talked to the Lieutenant Provost Marshal. There had been an assault and robbery and about eighty English pounds had been taken from the victim. My two soldiers were in the neighborhood so they were questioned; they had about the amount of money that was stolen.

This had happened right after pay day. Well, after pay day there are always some craps games, dice rolling. Some men go away a little richer, and some go away a little broker. With this information I went back to Cheltenham and told the 1st Sergeant to get all the men in who had been in a dice game after pay day. Then we had to see who was playing in which games. Not everybody shoots dice, and among the dice players not all of them will play with certain people. Since I was not a dedicated gambler of any kind, I was learning stuff that I knew nothing about.

After a number of trial-and-error questionings, each group that had been down on their knees seeking more wealth had been identified. I finally found two groups that remembered the two men. Both groups remembered that the Sergeant and the Private seemed to be having a run of luck. By the time we had finished questioning the dice groups and added up what it looked like the men could have won with what the Paymaster had delivered to them, they would have had about the amount that the victim said had been taken from him.

I went back to Taunton and talked to the Provost Marshal and showed him what we thought had gone on. The Provost Marshal said it looked like we had put enough evidence together to clear my two soldiers. He also said, considering the time and effort that we had put into trying to solve this problem, he was going to turn them over to me to take back to their outfit. If anything more came of it, he would let me know, and he also said if he ever got into trouble he would like me to be on his side.

■ ■ ■

April came and my second wedding anniversary was coming up, too. Out of twenty-four months of married life, I had gotten to live with my beautiful wife for four months. Each time birthdays and anniversaries came by, I turned blue for a few days, and then the amount of work that had to be done would soon shake the blues off.

Abruptly I was transferred to a new department, new job, new Commanding Officer. On April 18 I was transferred out of my beloved infantry company into Headquarters Command, ETOUSA, which was a good-sized headquarters that had charge of all the officers and enlisted men who did all of the inside and outside work that was required for Services of Supply, G-4 ETOUSA. I reported to my new Commanding Officer, Colonel C. S. Turner, and he acquainted me with my new job.

He said to me, "Captain Mayhall, you will be a member of my staff. We already have a Chief of Staff, and S-1, S-3, S-4. You will be the S-2. You will do the intelligence work—that will be your department. You will read all information that comes in that refers to the S-2 Department; and if you think it is some-

Above: Invasion rehearsal. (FDR Library)

thing that should come to my attention, give it to the Chief of Staff, and then after he reads it, if he thinks I should see it, he will give it to me. In the meantime you will be doing whatever S-2s do."

That last statement sort of shook me, because so far all I knew about S-2s was that they were rather hard to find most of the time. The ones that I knew back in the regiment always seemed to be in a hurry.

At first I hated being transferred from my regiment into the big Headquarters. But it put me in a place where I could learn staff work, which beforehand I had never had any desire to do. I met people from all different jobs preparing for the invasion of France. The troops themselves really didn't care where supplies came from or who loaded or unloaded them, so long as the supplies were there when they needed them.

Someone had set up a little spy system in some of the units supporting this large Headquarters. The S-2 Department had an active agent in the Communication Unit, Engineering Unit, Transportation Unit, and some of the others. I got a report regularly from each one of these agents. Everything went well until one of my little agents was sitting in a meeting with his Chief of Section, who happened to be the bird colonel who was head of the Communication Unit. In talking to his group, the Colonel gave a hint as to when D-Day was going to come off. Nobody, I mean Nobody, made references to D-Day. The report got to me, and I whistled it right on up the chain of command, and that made lots of heads bump together. It finally got to General Weaver, who called the Colonel in and had a very serious talk about the Colonel's going home. When the General got through with him, he had to unzip his mouth to say hello.

■ ■ ■

My next little experience was with a British secretary who had worked for the secret agency MI-5. She came into our headquarters looking for someone she could talk to about some information she had. It was important that it got to the right people. This lady was bounced around until she got to me. I wondered what she could tell me and what I could do with it if any big information came out of it. So I arranged for a private room, and we moved into it.

First off the lady needed a cup of tea and cigarettes. I made arrangements for this and then sat back with pencil and paper to make notes. She talked and talked about herself and her family, and after about four hours I began to wonder where all the important stuff was. Maybe I had been missing it. But I hadn't heard anything that sounded like MI-5. MI-5 did unfunny stuff like dropping people in France to meet with the French underground, and dropping dead people off of submarines with chains on their wrists attached to an attaché case with papers that had near truths in them. MI-5 had numbers of very sophisticated, very secret projects going on that nobody else should have known about.

So I am sitting with my ears pointed at the lady and nothing was going on. No explosions, no secret agents, no German spies. I began to think this lady was having some problems. Thank goodness, I was called out of the room by a group of people looking for her. It turned out that she had worked too long and too hard and had suffered a serious breakdown. People with breakdowns in a lot of cases look just as normal as anyone else. She was being nursed in a quiet hospital that housed a number of persons trying to get over the pressure of the war. The people talked very nicely to the lady and told her it was tea time and it was time to go back.

I met another group during this S-2 experience. I met them in one of the offices in the headquarters. All of them were in uniform of different ranks. They were a very pleasant group; we talked and laughed. As time went on, I went to restaurants and places where civilians and soldiers mixed, and one of these people would show up in civilian clothes and wouldn't seem to know me at all. I finally decided here were our secret agents, from the Office of Strategic Services. Normally, when I saw a familiar face in an odd place we went back to the room in Headquarters, where we laughed and talked and caught up with each other. The last thing an S-2 would like to be dumb enough to do is to blow somebody's cover. These people showed up in so many places where I happened to be, I wondered if maybe they were doing a background check on *me*.

■ ■ ■

"Tell Anybody Hello"

I felt that this transfer into the S-2 business was my first step toward active combat. In the 156th Infantry it looked like I would never get into a division in combat. I had been anxious to get to Europe. But the closer I got, the less anxious I was. It was the same sort of caution one feels as one drives into denser fog, the same feeling you get as you move from a lighted area into a darker one.

D-Day came crashing down upon all of us. The tension was so great, so thick you could almost slice it. We could hardly keep from jumping and hollering when planes pulling large gliders passed overhead. Great formations of B-187s and many, many fighter planes all were heading east toward France.

As S-2 Headquarters Command, ETOUSA, I was allowed to sit in on the intelligence briefing each morning given by the G-2 for the information of General Lee and his G-4 staff. I got to know the G-2, and he told me that I might as well bring the people that I had working for me into his G-2 room and brief them there instead of trying to carry my things someplace else. The people in my group were very impressed with the pictures of the beaches of burnt-out tanks, shot-up assault boats, the many soldiers who had been killed. They were very much interested in the maps that showed the progress of forward movement. On the intelligence maps and pictures I saw the Third Army, committed under the command of General Patton, break out after a massive bombing attack on Saint Lô, plowing, shooting through what was left of the city.

Above: American Wounded, D-Day. (FDR Library)

It was exciting to everyone in England, whether he was a postal clerk, cook, typist, or truck driver. The only way home for us was across the English Channel, across France, and across as much of Germany as necessary. Everyone did his job, and when D-Day arrived everyone felt that he was part of it, whatever he was doing or wherever he was. Because of the number of casualties on the beaches, some of the soldiers who were working in England found themselves in Replacement Depots for retraining to combat infantry. Some were happy about this, and some were not.

Things changed again for me.

On June 21 I was transferred from the staff of Headquarters Command, ETOUSA, to Camp A ETOUSA. Camp A was just one hell of a beehive of people. There were twelve thousand soldiers housed and rationed in this complex. It was called the "Race Course." It was rather easy to figure out where the name came from—it was a race course. All the stables were cleaned out; the clubhouse and everything about a race course that has a roof had troops under it. How I got the Race Course command is another little story.

What happened between the former Commander—a 1st Lieutenant—and his 1st Sergeant I don't know. But all of a sudden the 1st Lieutenant decided to court-martial his 1st Sergeant. So the 1st Lieutenant started collecting information that he could take to court. Well, it turned out that the 1st Sergeant was an old soldier, had been in the Army a long time. The 1st Sergeant went to the Judge Advocate General section where he had some friends. The JAG began to look into the situation, and they turned up enough information on the 1st Lieutenant that it would be embarrassing for the action against the 1st Sergeant to go any further.

So what happened? The JAG must have thought: "Who do we have in the Headquarters staff with troop experience? Why, Captain Mayhall. He's been commanding an infantry company. He's tough. He knows what to do with 1st Sergeants. We'll put Captain Mayhall out there in charge of that camp, and he'll straighten out that 1st Sergeant in a hurry." So there went my staff job. I was just beginning to enjoy S-2 work. What was worse was that June 6 and D-Day had come and gone. In the S-2 position I had been invited to the G-2 update of what was happening on the beaches in France and all of the advances on the maps. The Race Course was so busy it was hard to find out what was going on anywhere else.

I was disappointed, but it was never a matter of liking or disliking any new assignment; every person did his job to support the overall effort. This was "seven to one" again: seven people behind the lines to put one man on the front.

I went to the 1st Sergeant and sat down with him and told him that if he would mind his business, I would try to mind mine. At this same time, the 1st Sergeant explained to me some of the things going on at the Race Course. It seemed the Race Course was a quick stopping place for special troops coming from the States. The large port of Brest had been captured and had to be put back in condition for the Allies to use. So welding teams came through, picked up their equipment, and were off to port of embarkation, with carpenter teams, telephone men, radio men, warehousemen, crane operators, and men who knew how to dock boats. It was necessary to get Brest open to bring in supplies in large enough amounts to keep the armies moving.

The move from S-2 to Camp Commander of Camp A was another learning experience. There were 12,000 people in this "way station," involved in the rebuilding and operation of the port of Cherbourg. The Germans had tried to destroy Cherbourg to keep the Americans and British from using it. Our forces needed the port very badly—we couldn't get enough supplies over the beaches.

My next step toward active participation in the war in France was on July 17. General Weaver came nose to nose with Colonel Turner and told him to have Mayhall transferred into his section and have me report for duty in the morning. Now I was "G-1 Liaison to the Field Coordinator." I think General Weaver asked for me because, being an infantry officer himself, he liked having infantry people around him. He had been to inspect my Company many times to watch our training exercises.

I was told that I would go to London once a week and talk to the G-1 section in London, find out what was going on, and report to General Weaver what I did on my trips. In addition, I was to help General Weaver plan trips here and there for his job as Field Coordinator to General Lee. He was what we would call a troubleshooter. When there was a supply stoppage anywhere in England, General Weaver showed up to get that line of supply unstopped. This didn't mean a half pound of ham for supper, but tons of food, ammunition, tanks, trucks, halftracks, airplanes, airplane parts, artillery, and men. I had a good job; I didn't work hard, but I learned a lot about supply. I met a whole lot of people who later turned up on the front pages of newspapers.

It was during this that time the Germans perfected the "Buzz Bomb" V-1 weapon. The Buzz Bomb was a flying bomb that looked like a torpedo with short wings, and was propelled by a motor called a ram jet. It was launched from a ground rack that looked like a long shoot-D-chute that pointed it into the air in the direction of London. It only had fuel enough to get to the London area. It was a very effective weapon, and for a long time it was very nerve wracking. As time wore on, we learned where they were launched and we bombed the launching sites. The British learned to shoot them down, which was not easy because the fighter plane had to be in position to dive on the Buzz Bomb

Above: View of a V-1 rocket in flight over a London rooftop, 1944. (National Archives, NWDNS-306-NT-3157V)

as soon as it was spotted. Antiaircraft guns got some of them, but they didn't seem to get any on the days that I was in London.

I saw as many as five Buzz Bombs come by in a day. Everybody that could hear it would stop and listen, hoping the noise would go by—hoping the motor didn't shut off before it passed where they were. The noise of the ram jet was like a large tractor passing by. When the noise of the motor stopped, the Buzz Bomb headed to the ground. There were enough explosives in it to flatten a quarter of a block.

General Weaver was in London in a hotel when one of those bombs came in close. He was shaving—the window in the bathroom was blown in and the General was showered with glass. It drew blood, but he said hell no, that wasn't the way he would take a Purple Heart. He would go to Europe on a stretcher if necessary.

About this time (summer of 1944) General Eisenhower gave Louisiana State University, Baton Rouge, and Louisiana a great big pat on the back. There was an officer who had been head of the Cadet Corps at LSU who was in the First World War, who had become acquainted with a lot of WWI officers such as Generals Hodges, Simpson, Patton, Walker, and Weaver. This officer was General Troy H. Middleton; he was so well respected that, when he was to be kept in the States for one reason or another, General Eisenhower gave orders to bring him back to the London area. General Middleton's arrival in Europe put me another little bit closer to active combat.

General Middleton had known General Weaver very well during WWI. WWI was the breeding ground for the great generals of WWII. The 90th Infantry Division—the Texas-Oklahoma "Tough 'Ombres"—was having trouble on the beaches. They were considered a problem division with poor leadership at various levels and with a poor showing under fire. As a result of this trouble, the Division Commander, Assistant Division Commander, and eighteen field officers were relieved. General Middleton seemed to be the officer to put it back together. So he picked a General McLain as Division Commander and he got to looking for a fighting general for Assistant Division Commander. He knew General Weaver was in the ETO and sent out a call for him. Well, General Weaver was as happy as he could be. He was afraid that he might have to fight this war from behind the lines.

When he got ready to leave Cheltenham, he asked me, "Mayhall, you want to go?"

I came back with an answer so fast it surprised me. "General, that's what I have been training three years for." I knew I didn't want to stay where I was if General Weaver wasn't going to be there.

The General said, "I'll send for you."

General Weaver was given a farewell party on the 26th of July and left without me. The next I heard of him, he was with "Hell for Leather" Task Force Weaver. He was running the 90th Infantry Division east across France in order to get ahead of the German 7th Army trying to get out of the Falaise Gap—leading one of the point task forces that was heading Patton's 3rd Army. Task Force Weaver was the unit closest to the 7th Army's flank.

General Weaver sent back on August 2 for my full name and serial number. I began to think he hadn't forgotten me after all. I knew his aide had been wounded, to say nothing of the fact that he had been shot as well. General Weaver did not consider his own leg wound reason enough to go back to the Aid Station. He just got a first-aid man to wrap it up for him.

General MacKelvie, who had been relieved of command of the 90th Division, was sent back to England and put to work doing what General Weaver had been doing, Field Coordinator for General Lee. General MacKelvie was an artillery officer and a good one; but as an Infantry Division Commander, he seemed to be out of his league. He did the Field Coordinator job just until a Division Artillery Officer was needed, and back to France he went.

I didn't see much of General MacKelvie in spite of the fact that we were in the same wing and his office was just down the hall from mine. He spent his time moving around England getting familiar with his new job. We had a full Colonel who was Chief-of-Staff under the Field Coordinator, so he gave us orders, and we reported to him. One morning he called me in and said, "Mayhall, I have a circular here that says they want some officers to go home and go to Command and General Staffs School."

Knowing I didn't have enough schools, I became very interested. I was as interested in getting more training as in getting into battle. I said, "Sounds good, but General Weaver said he would send for me."

The Colonel said, "Well, let's put it like this: We will put your name down to go home, and whichever comes in first takes it."

I thought it sounded great until one of our smiling sergeants knocked on the door and came in. "Guess what. Captain Mayhall has been requested to report to the 90th Infantry Division."

The Sergeant handed the TPX to the Colonel, who said, "Looks like the question of where you are going has been decided."

Some change in scenery would have happened to me one way or another. Shortly after I left for France, B Company was pulled back together with the rest of the Regiment and assigned to as many different jobs in France as they had been in England. Some were used to keep the Germans on Guernsey Island

Below: Corporal Charles H. Johnson of the 783rd Military Police Battalion waves on a Red Ball Express motor convoy rushing to the forward areas. Near Alendon, France, September 5, 1944. (National Archives, NWDNS-111-SC-195512)

off the coast of France. Some were detailed to guard the Red Ball route from the coast to the front. As the demand for replacements for frontline units became acute, sixty percent of the old regiment went to Replacement Depots and were replaced in the regiment with people wounded too bad to go back to the front but not bad enough to go home.

I was to report to the Replacement Depot at Litchfield as soon as I could get there. I packed and was off the next day. I wandered around the Repl' Depo' for a couple of days and watched as new officers and enlisted men came in straight from the States along with an influx of men and officers coming back from hospitals. We were broken down into groups that would fit on the trains and boats.

It took three days to get a train from Litchfield to Tidworth, where I had spent my first assignment. Tidworth had changed considerably. It had been a rather small supply depot, but now it was a big, busy replacement center where one could get on a boat for France in a hurry. There was a big mess hall that would feed a battalion at a time. From Tidworth we were railroaded to the port. The next morning I was on a boat heading for France.

We spent the night on the boat, and the next evening we disembarked and went up to the beach. We reached "Omaha Red" very quickly. There were no signs that a hell of a battle had been fought getting on this beach and getting to the high land where the Germans were throwing everything they had down on the GIs. It was quiet as we walked up the beach and into an apple orchard, where there were thousands of tons of canned food, bombs, ammunition waiting to catch up with the battlefields.

There was a young Lieutenant there to direct us to where we would stay for the night. We were told that trucks would arrive in the morning to take us to the next replacement center. Our first night in France was spent sleeping on the ground. There were no snakes cozying up to get warm, never saw a spider—the only unfriendlies were Germans.

The Lieutenant who had met us turned out to be Lt. Wybra S. DeLaune, who had left B Company to go off to OCS. He had left just before I took command of the Company. Lt. DeLaune had been a very popular noncom in B Company, and he left a lot of friends when he went to OCS. He wanted to know where the company was, what they had been doing, how many more went off to OCS. I filled him in on the activities of the company, and he filled me in on what he had been doing since he graduated from OCS. When I climbed onto the truck to leave, he shouted, "Tell anybody hello!"

The next day was bright and clear. I was a little surprised that we couldn't hear any cannon fire. Everyone was in a hurry to collect their stuff to be ready when the trucks arrived. I went up close enough to the food stacks and saw that they were large cans of turkey. It occurred to me that I might not see any more turkey for a long time, so I helped out the problem of transporting all this stuff by taking a can myself.

The can of turkey and I went forward to the next Replacement Depot. We drove to the famous Saint Lô where the fighting had been so bitter. I showed the orders that I carried with me and I didn't even get my bed roll on the ground before I was put on a convoy going forward that night.

The convoy was not leaving from the Replacement Depot itself, but it would be passing a crossroads seven or eight miles away. They loaded me on a jeep and dropped me and my bed roll at the crossroads. It wasn't a very busy crossroads. As a matter of fact, nothing passed that crossroads for three or four hours. My thoughts went back to those maps in the G-2's office, to how rapidly the 3rd Army had run through this part of France and to the possibility of German stragglers still wandering around trying to get back to a larger unit. A .45-caliber automatic is very good company; so I loaded it with one shell in the chamber, hammer back on safety. I began to wonder what a German halftrack sounded like; all of a sudden I didn't know what one of our $2\frac{1}{2}$-ton tracks sounded like. I loaded my carbine and put it on safety, also.

I began to hear trucks. I couldn't see any; they were back down in the woods. The sound of motors was getting louder, and I was getting closer to the ground. Finally, the first truck broke out into the open, and I was so glad to see that olive drab and white star. I jumped up and started waving, and the men in the

Above: Infantrymen line up in front of a wrecked German tank and display a captured flag in Chambois, France, last stronghold of the Nazis in the Falaise Gap. August 20, 1944. (National Archives, NWDNS-112-SGA-44(12123))

first truck waved back as they went by. The same with the second, third, and fourth truck. They waved and kept on going. The last truck was the only one that seemed to realize I was out there waiting for them, and as it slowed down a guy stood up on the back of the truck and started shouting. He seemed to be very excited. Finally I began to understand he was shouting, "Hey, Van! Hey, Van!"

I wondered who in the world this could be. This wasn't Third Street, Baton Rouge—not too many would recognize me out here at the crossroads in midwestern France. The truck stopped, and I threw my stuff up on top and climbed up, and there was Lieutenant Sidney Champagne, whom I had known most of my life. He was a couple of years behind me at Catholic High, so I wondered what a young fellow like him was doing out here with the grown-up people. I had to accept that some of my young friends had grown up. Sidney had finished Catholic High, finished LSU, and was commissioned through the ROTC. Now he had caught up with me.

We rode along on top of that truck until we got to the next Replacement Depot, south of Paris at a place named Fontainbleau. It was a big depot. There were about 5000 replacement officers and men there. Lieutenant Sidney Champagne and I pitched our shelter halves close by and talked about home and the war.

I had been away from home since December 1940, so he knew a lot of news which I was glad to hear. This was a celebration so we broke out the can of turkey and warmed it by the fire.

We had a little bit of enemy action—"Bed Check Charlie," a German plane that flew over Fontainbleau with some regularity. The plane didn't make any hostile acts and we didn't do any shooting at the plane. Doris Day came to sing for me and my 5000 associates. I wasn't close enough to see anything more than that she was sort of blondish, but I could tell her voice was beautiful.

Lieutenant Sidney Champagne and I spent two or three days visiting, talking, and throwing bayonets. He was wondering where he was going. I knew where I was going. I had direct orders for the 90th Infantry Division. Paris wasn't but about twenty miles away, so some of our group decided we would go visit. Sidney wouldn't go because he didn't know when his group would go forward. The group that I went to Paris with were some of the people who had been wounded and were on their way back to their units.

Off to Paris we went, and wandered around for three days. I saw the Eiffel Tower, Arc de Triomphe and the wide busy streets, the Seine River, and Notre Dame. The cathedral had always been in the back of my mind because I had seen the "Hunchback of Notre Dame" more than once.

The people in Paris were good to us. They would crowd around us to hear us talk. I never paid for a meal in any restaurant. The people wanted to look at us, listen to us, and hear us try to speak French. There was no reason why I couldn't speak

French. I had studied it for two years at Catholic High, and I saw those little kids in Paris who hadn't even started school speaking it.

After the visit to Paris I caught a ride back to Fontainbleau. Sidney and his group had already gone forward. Since Sidney had been the only person there I knew, I decided I ought to go forward also, but first I went up to the chateau and looked around inside. It was beautiful. I am sure that a lot of us men could have been billeted there, but they kept it all for the Repl' Depo' officers and their help and for visiting dignitaries. Generals and people from Washington couldn't be expected to spend their nights out on the ground under a pup tent with all us heroes.

I checked to see if my orders had caught up through channel yet. The answer was no, so I pulled out my own copy of my orders and I was on my way forward riding in the back of a shell truck that night with three other soldiers. The truck's load of 155mm shells was being delivered right to the 90th Infantry's area.

One of the other people on the truck was a returnee, a sergeant on his way back to the outfit that he belonged to before he was wounded. The hospital had sewn him up and his wound was not serious enough for him to be sent back to the States. So he was put in rehabilitation and at some point someone said he was ready to go back and here he was on top of a shell truck heading to the front lines into "harm's way."

Somewhere on the ride the sergeant pulled out a bottle of whiskey and was generous enough to pass it around. It was much appreciated. One of the things that I had left off of my packing list was one or two bottles of some kind of drinking stuff. I saw now that it would have been an important travelling aid in this part of France.

We had passed Paris and were heading east. I was glad my bed roll was travelling with me. Sitting on the bed roll was a lot better than trying to get comfortable on the pointed end of one of those 155mm projectiles.

■ ■ ■

Battlefield Grey

Somewhere east of Paris I began to hear a rumble. It sounded like a far-off thunderstorm. The farther east the convoy travelled, the louder the thunder got, and soon enough I had changed my mind about this rumble being a storm. The front lines ran for miles to our left and right. The 8-inch guns, 155mm guns, and 105mm guns were firing. That was the rumble.

I was dropped off at the 90th Division Rear somewhere in the area of a little French town called Doncourt. There was much excitement. There had been a big battle the night before and people in Division Rear didn't know what had happened—was the fighting still going on and was Division Rear going to be involved? This did not make me feel any better about my introduction to the 90th Infantry. The 90th had recently recovered from its poor reputation—General Omar Bradley had considered them a "problem division" when they first landed at Normandy. General "Wild Bill" Weaver had been a welcome change in Assistant Division Commander. He wasn't one to command from a safe place far behind the lines. He was even a bit reckless, as I would discover firsthand.

A guy with a paintbrush and stencil came up to me and said, "Captain, let me have your left shoulder." I turned my left side toward him and before I knew what he was doing, I had a T and O—

ᴛ⊖

—painted on my shirt. The man said, "Captain, you are now a Tough 'Ombre."

145

I joined the group of people who had just come up, and it seemed that, being it was about 10:00 P.M., we might as well bed down. I pitched my pup tent, crawled in, laid my rifle close to my right hand, undid the top of my leggings to loosen them a little, and undid my belt-top button on my pants. I had no idea how near or far the fighting was. I lay down on my back and placed my .45 on my stomach and closed my eyes, and was happy in the morning to find I hadn't shot myself while I was asleep.

I located the food line and enjoyed some breakfast. It wasn't long before someone came through shouting my name. The word had gotten to the General that I was at Division Rear, so he had sent one of his drivers to pick me up. I did the best I could to straighten up my appearance. I learned what dry shaving was all about—you took out your razor and scraped the whiskers off, with or without soap and water and shaving cream. I got to Division Headquarters in time for lunch with the General and his staff, and sat and listened.

I was certainly glad to see someone I knew. I respected General Weaver. He was like a good book waiting to be written—the way he had served in past wars, had found a way overseas, and had rebuilt the Division and led his task force. Under Generals McLain and Weaver, the 90th Division was finally getting respect, too.

The excitement that had given the Division Rear the jitters had been quite a battle. A German brigade was travelling southwest to relieve another German unit and had come into the 90th Division area over a road that had not been protected. The head of their column got to the 90th Division Headquarters before they were discovered, and all hell broke loose.

General Weaver had been in his bed roll when the fireworks started. He ran outside of his tent and climbed into one of our tanks, and they went around shooting at whatever looked German. The division sort of turned inside out and killed or captured the whole brigade. Our people didn't get off light. A number of officers were killed in their sleeping bags. A number of our people were wounded by friendly fire. People moving around in the dark don't make good targets, but they do get shot at.

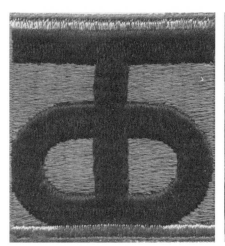

Above, left: 90th Division "Tough 'Ombres" shoulder patch. Above right: General Weaver flanked by his orderly, Garman, (left) and driver, Perko (right). Below: Infantrymen of the 255th Infantry Regiment move down a street in Waldenburg. (National Archives, NWDNS-111-SC-205778)

After lunch the General told Perko, his driver, to take me down and show me all those "good" Germans. "Yes*sir*, sir," he said and we climbed into a jeep and drove off. I didn't see the General's car—not that I had too many thoughts about the Packard! I saw plenty of jeeps, tanks, tank destroyers with 90mm guns, $2\frac{1}{2}$-ton trucks, no gasoline trucks (they were supplying General Montgomery's "Bridge Too Far"). I liked seeing the tanks, tank destroyers, and all that artillery. It made me feel I wasn't alone.

This village we were going to had been one of the areas fought over the night before. It was really something. I saw one of our rifles standing with the butt straight up with an American helmet on it. Before I could ask Perko explained, "That's one of our people the graves registration hasn't gotten to yet." As we came to the edge of the small village, the scene took on the look of a Hollywood war movie.

It was certainly war. There were dead German soldiers lying in the street, on the curbs, on steps, hanging half out of windows. There was no place you could look in this little village that you would not see young Germans lying dead. It was my first experience with battlefield grey. I had been to many funerals at home, but I had never seen a body without makeup. Battlefield grey is easy to recognize, and there is something very sad about it no matter what uniform you wear. At the time I had no remorse at seeing all of these dead Krauts who for sure would not shoot at any of us again. On the way back to headquarters I had only one thought: "You sure have gotten Mrs. Mayhall's little boy in harm's way."

We got back to General Weaver's trailer. A first-aid soldier was on his way out. He had just changed the bandage on the General's leg. He apparently didn't think I looked too faint after seeing battle dead for the first time. We talked a little while, and he told me the General's former aide had taken a bullet in the stomach and probably would not come back from the hospital. His former driver had developed a rash of some kind and he had written the General that he would not come back because all that tension, noise, and exploding shells made the rash worse. They had put him to work in the rear.

So the General now had John Perko as a driver and John Garman as his man's man. Garman saw to it the General had something to wear. Perko made it a point to keep the General off of those "88mm boulevards"—roads under enemy bombardment—which were very unhealthy for both of them.

The General acquainted me with the part of this 90th Infantry Division I would be added to. It seems that I had been recommended as a fine Company Commander, so I was assigned to C Company, 357th Infantry. The idea way in the back of my mind that I would be added to the General's staff died on the vine. Transportation arrangements were made and I joined C Company just as they were moving into a little town called Neufchef. The only action was when a German sniper who had been left behind killed one of the head men in our column. The town was supposed to have been clear.

I met the Battalion Commander and was sent down to the Company. Lieutenant Phyffer was very glad to see me. He was the only officer left in C Company. He had outlived two Company Commanders already, and he didn't want to be Company Commander himself. I met the 1st Sergeant, who also had outlived the last two Company Commanders. I had been a Company Commander for so long before I got to France that I easily busied myself with what was going on now—how many people did we have, what were we doing right now?

At the moment the company and battalion were doing what they did every night—they had picked a place they thought they could defend and began to set up all-around defense. It was not expected that we would be attacked, so the kitchen crews were trying to cook hot food. Men were bringing up bed rolls for the squads. The 1st Sergeant and Lieutenant Phyffer had set up company headquarters in a two-story house, and most of us were downstairs in one room. The 1st Sergeant told me that there was a bed upstairs, but not to expect to get much sleep because around dark the Germans started shelling us with a battery of 105mms. They didn't hit anybody or anything, but it did keep us wondering where the next shells would land.

The next day we were to take a village called Hayange sitting down between two high hills. Company C would take the

hill on the right (south) and A Company would take the hill on
the left (north). We called the north hill Statue Hill because it
had a statue of Our Lady thirty feet high on it. Night passed
and there we were, ready to get on with the job. Word got to me
that one of the C Company sergeants was missing. We waited
about one good breath for the sergeant and we took off for our
hill. As we were passing the last house, the sergeant made his
appearance.

Even from the distance I saw he had a snoot full of whiskey.
It looked like he intended to keep the level on his snoot where
it was because he had two tall bottles, one under each arm. I
had some thoughts about how a fellow could get hurt going into
attack full of liquid. What does the book on courts martial have
to say about this sort of happy living? The sergeant fell in with
his platoon without any more ado. I did not hear any more from
the sergeant, and the platoon he was in did the job they were
supposed to—so no problem.

The hill that we were taking had a lot of tall trees growing
on it—practically had no underbrush. What was more important, there were no Germans defending it, so we walked on and
developed a perimeter defense and started digging in. In the
meantime the Germans had a battery of 105mm guns in range
of our hill. They began to shell us. It seemed just like some of
the maneuvers I had been on in the States. One hears the
artillery go off and hears the shell coming and hits the ground
until the shell bursts.

I moved around trying to check the platoons. Then I decided
I should find a place to dig a hole. I wanted a place where I could
see more than one direction. Being green, I chose a gap in a
hedgerow. I could look across the valley where A Company was
having a mean fight trying to get Statue Hill, and through the
gap in the hedgerow in the direction from which the Germans
were shelling us. Not only did it have a clear view in both directions, the ground seemed to be soft there. So I started digging.
As I dug it seemed the Germans were getting more familiar.
They passed some of those shells so close to that spot I could
smell them as they went by. After a while I got to wondering
where that sergeant was with those two long bottles. I didn't

Above: Soldiers take cover from enemy sniper fire. (US Army Military History Institute)

Above: American howitzers shell German forces retreating near Carentan, France. July 11, 1944. (National Archives, NWDNS-111-SC-191933)

know until the next day that the Germans had the gaps in the hedgerows zeroed in on their fire plans, so I was sitting in the middle of a reference point.

Night passed and the 1st Sergeant reported that we had one Killed In Action. The Sergeant who I had ridden on the shell truck with had received a direct hit from one of those 105s. I felt a little sad, for this was the only man in C Company that I came near knowing.

A Company had not been very lucky on Statue Hill. They met dug-in resistance and some SS troops had joined the defense. A Company got chewed up pretty good. Since C Company had only one KIA, the Battalion Commander pulled A Company out and decided to send C Company up to get Statue Hill the following morning. C Company settled into attack position at the bottom of the hill. There we were lined up across the bottom of the hill, and the Artillery Support Officer says to me, "Captain, I see movement on top of the hill, but I don't think they are German soldiers." I asked what civilians would be doing up there. He said, "They're looking for whatever they can find—money, cigarettes, food."

I didn't like the sound of robbing the dead. "Move the top of the hill," I told him. The officer ordered for artillery fire on the hill. It didn't take but a very few shells for the people on top of the hill to disappear. In the meantime C Company had started moving. There was no more movement from the hilltop, and not a single rifle was fired at us. As we headed up the hill, we were sure the Germans would pop up and start shooting at any time. However, the closer we got to the top of the hill, the more we became certain instead that the Germans had pulled off.

As we got about halfway up the hill, my radio sergeant said, "Captain, there's a woman in one of those houses broadcasting information." I didn't understand German, but he did, and this German woman was broadcasting our position and what size unit we had. Thank goodness the Germans didn't have any guns set up in position to fire on us. Those 105mms that had been firing on us the day before must have been pulled back. The German woman who was broadcasting had put herself in harm's way. Anybody in the company would have taken pleasure in shooting her. We turned the information over to the Intelligence Officer and went on. Thank goodness the Germans had pulled out. The side of the hill we were going up was more like your front yard—no dips, ditches, or rolls in the ground to get into if the shooting started.

We got to the top of Statue Hill and set up security and started digging in. We found the A Company people who didn't come down off the hill the night before—they couldn't; they had all been killed. One shell came in during the three days we stayed there doing nothing. That was all right. We were getting hot meals, had a chance to count noses, and I finally found out we had one more officer. He was the Weapon's Platoon Leader, and he had done a good job for a long time.

I was willing to stay where we were for a few more days. I had learned the 1st Sergeant's name. I knew what some of the noncom platoon leaders looked like, and I knew Lieutenant Phyffer, and I had met the Weapon's Platoon Leader two or three times, though his name never did stick.

Everything was too good where we were.

I heard trucks at a distance and soon the order came down, "Hurry up to move." Not having anything but my rifle and pistol, it wasn't hard to get ready. We hadn't found out where we were going yet, but we were on the way. I don't know how far we went, but it was nearly dark when we got there. The battalion set to work developing all-around security and foxholes to sleep in. The Company Commanders were called back to Battalion Headquarters just after dark, and we were idling around waiting for the last Company Commander to get there when the Germans began shelling the area we were in. There were no foxholes around, no big trucks—just one little jeep! I thought I was pretty fast but by the time I came plowing up to that jeep, all there was room for under it was for my head.

The Company Commanders remained at Battalion Headquarters for the night. I don't know why, unless they had lost a few Company Commanders wandering around in the dark looking for their Company Headquarters.

The Battalion Commander let us know we had come to the Metz area to relieve the 7th Armored Division. The Germans were eating them up in this hill country. The Germans were knocking out their tanks with *panzerfaust,* a hand-operated weapon for close-up work. We pulled some of the 7th Armored wounded people out of their hiding places and got them back to medical aid. The hills and valleys in front of Group Lorraine (a huge fort that protected the northwest approaches of Metz) were not for tanks.

I guess General Weaver knew considerable much about new people in the front line. He sent me to that little town to see all those "good" Krauts and from then on, I had very little feeling about somebody getting killed or wounded. Even the soldier that I knew, the sergeant who I rode on the shell truck with, I never had a second thought about him. It was just what happened to people in the front lines. They were in harm's way.

Our little battle at Hayange was over with, and we had been moved to the next point where we were needed. The 7th Armored Division needed to be pulled out of the line to refit and replace. After relieving the 7th Armored, we got the orders to attack Group Lorraine. Our first information about Group Lorraine was that it was a strongly protected fort and it was supposed to have a concrete wall around it twenty feet high and thirty feet thick. C Company would be the first to attack and capture a stone quarry that the Germans had been defending which was in plain view of the fort. This would be day one attack on Group Lorraine. After we had captured the stone quarry, C Company was to turn east and attack the fort.

■ ■ ■

Opposite: Soldiers of Battery C, 557th A.A.A. AW Battalion man a .50-caliber mobile antiaircraft gun. (US Army Military History Institute)

First Day Attack on Group Lorraine

When daylight broke it was foggy and visibility was not very good. Word came down from Battalion that the Germans had pulled out of the stone quarry and C Company was to send a strong combat patrol to secure it. During the night a replacement lieutenant had arrived. Tall, blue-eyed, blond, and every a bit a man. He ran up to me and wanted to lead the combat patrol. It seemed that he was afraid this war was going to be over before he had gotten a chance to be in it. He wanted part of it. I sent him with the patrol.

It wasn't long before I received a message from him saying the stone quarry was secure and he was going across the road to check out the two or three little buildings there. While I was reading his note there was a loud explosion from the direction he had gone with his Platoon Sergeant and one or two other men. The Lieutenant had opened a door and there was a *click*. The Sergeant shouted a warning but the Lieutenant didn't have time to get out of the way. The Sergeant and the men with him had turned and dived out of the way, but the Lieutenant caught the full blast of the booby trap. He was wounded badly.

In the meantime all of C Company had moved down into the quarry area. The loud explosion of the booby trap had awakened the Germans, and they commenced to fire at everything that wiggled. I was sitting up on the inside rim of the stone quarry watching the goings on. I suppose I should have had some little bushes stuck in my helmet netting, but I didn't. A German who was firing a machine gun up there thought there might be someone under the American helmet. Fortunately his windage was off a little bit, and he just kicked sandstone all in my face. I didn't let him get in another shot. There were other places for me to go.

I went across the road. The 1st Platoon had begun to work their way toward the fort, which we still couldn't see. The area that C Company was supposed to attack near the fort was clean and clear, except for a few rolls in the ground for the platoon to take cover in. I radioed to battalion for permission to move to the left where there were woods and brush, which would give us more cover to move forward. This was okayed, and we moved except for a platoon pinned down by the machine-gun nest. We moved around to the left and opened fire on the machine-gun emplacement. There must have been some kind of protection for that nest. We didn't knock it out at all.

We got into the woods where artillery fire was heavy. We thought it was our artillery so we radioed for them to stop. It stopped all right, but we never did find out whose artillery it was. We checked to see if anyone got hit. One of the platoon runners said he thought that he had felt something a while before. He looked through his equipment until he got to the rubber part of his gas mask. There was a piece of shrapnel that would have made quite a hole in him if that gas mask hadn't been in the way.

The Germans had stopped shooting at the pinned-down platoon. As I watched, Lieutenant Phyffer came walking up the road. He had been back with Company Rear and didn't know what was going on. He stopped out in the open to talk to the first man he could see of the platoon. The Germans started shooting at him and Lieutenant Phyffer turned ninety degrees from where the bullets were coming from and started running. The bullets kicked up dirt behind his heels, punching holes in his pants legs that were flapping behind him as he ran, but the bullets never drew a drop of his blood. Lieutenant Phyffer was one of the bravest men I ever saw, but this experience did not help his already nervous condition.

The platoon that was pinned down out in the open got help from a Captain Redfoot who was on the Battalion Staff. He was part of the S-3 section (plans and training) and he wandered

Above: S/Sgt. Minicozzi and Pfc. Andy Masiero examine helmet and liner pierced by an enemy bullet. (US Army Military History Institute)

around helping units when he could. Captain Redfoot got into the foxhole with the Platoon Sergeant and started talking to our artillery and found out there were some 8-inch guns in position. The shell from that gun sounded big as a bathtub as it went over. He got them to start shooting over the fort and then started "walking" one shell after another until he had shells landing on the top of the fort. While the Germans were looking for cover, the pinned-down platoon slipped out and moved into the woods. One of the Sergeants in this platoon came in with his own story. He had lifted his head a little bit, and one of the German riflemen shot at him and hit his helmet. It knocked a hole in his helmet about as big as a 50-cent piece. The bullet powdered in between his helmet and helmet liner and went around and burned him on the neck. I asked him if he wanted another helmet, one without such a big hole, since it had started raining. He said, "Hell no, this is the one with my name on it."

We started moving up the hill and came to a railroad track. It looked like it would have a machine gun firing down the track, so four of us ran across. To our surprise there was a machine-gun nest right where we chose to cross. Three of the Germans threw up their hands and started shouting "*Kamerad.*" The fourth one grabbed a potato masher grenade and threw it, but he was in such a hurry he forgot to pull the string on it, and he got four holes in his chest for his trouble.

These captives were welcome because this was one of the ways to get information fresh from the enemy.

As we went on up the hill to the same level as the top of the fort, we thought for sure that we were about to do something unfriendly to them. We moved over the crest of the hill. We still had plenty of cover to move forward. As we got closer to the end of the cover, we came under heavy machine-gun and mortar fire. The machine-gun fire was about two feet off the ground; as long as you were closer to the ground, there was a good chance you wouldn't get chewed up. The mortar fire started down to my left and started walking straight in my direction. A man about four yards ahead of me got a case of panic and decided to get up and move back. As he turned in my direction the last mortar shell exploded about three yards to my left and a piece of shrapnel hit his shoulder and went through the side of his face. I thought the next mortar round would hit me. I could imagine that German turning the dial, firing, turning the dial, getting a little closer. But it never came. Two more mils of traverse on that mortar sight would have dropped the next one right down my eternity.

The Company Commander of A Company was pretty close to where I was, and I heard him order a squad to charge in the direction of the fort. They charged, and the Germans shot that squad down in very short order. My first-aid man picked up his Red Cross flag and walked out into the open to examine the squad. They were all dead. I fully expected to have a dead first-aid man out there also, but the Germans respected the Red Cross flag and his bravery.

When the first-aid man got back under cover the Germans in the fort decided to let us know they meant business. They commenced to fire everything they had. It was so heavy that A Company and C Company broke and began to retreat to the rear where there was more cover. They ran by me, and there I was wondering, *What do I do now?* After a little while, my Radio Sergeant said, "Captain, this might be a counterattack. We'd better get out of here." I told the Sergeant we better go get the Company and bring them back up. So we went back and got the Company, brought them back up, and told them to dig in.

Our new Lieutenant, who had come up the night before and headed the patrol to get the stone quarry, did not get to the aid station in time to save his life.

The digging in was further complicated by rain. It began to come down in barrelfuls. It was beginning to get dark, and it was time for the rear echelon to start bringing up bed rolls, food, and ammunition. There was about a sixty degree slope. Now with the rain we had a stream of mud sliding downhill.

Our support people brought up the blanket rolls. They had developed a way of rolling up the blankets and shelter halves together. In the morning they brought rations and took the blanket rolls back to the company supply area to keep for the next night. Rations, while one was getting shot at, were usually K rations. When we were in rest areas it was hot meals of some kind.

It wasn't a good night. One man put his shelter half up over his foxhole and the Germans shot it full of holes. But he was never hit. His shelter just didn't keep much rain off him.

■ ■ ■

On the second day of the battle to capture Group Lorraine we planned to finish the job. The intelligence people in the battalion briefing had given us the information that the fort was surrounded by a concrete wall twenty feet high and thirty feet thick. The whole battalion would attack, reinforced by engineers who would bring scaling ladders and shaped and satchel charges to blow open doors when we found them.

The engineers arrived. Each company had been reinforced with a section of heavy machine guns. The Germans in the meantime had done a little reinforcing of their own. They rolled up one of those dreaded 88mm guns.

Nothing started well. We began to move, trying to see something to shoot at or call artillery down on. The Germans were just raising hell with us. The machine-gun fire was still coming in, the mortar fire still came in, and the 88mm was scoring tree bursts right over our heads. One squad charged out of the woods. The Germans shot them down. Once again our medic picked up his flag with the Red Cross on it and went out to check on the men. Once again the Germans let him walk out and examine the men and walk back in. Once again he found them all dead. Not all of the German units would allow a man to walk around with a Red Cross flag.

Below: Men attempt to dig free a tank bogged down in the mud during the drive into Germany. (US Army Military History Institute)

The attack was called off. The word was to dig in and hold. We didn't have to dig in, because we hadn't gone anywhere. When we had settled down to see what we were going to do next, I received word from battalion to send a reconnaissance patrol out to pick up whatever information they could. They were gone a couple of hours and came back to report they had seen the twenty-foot wall, had seen a door, and even saw a German go into the door.

At the time I thought this was good information. I was thinking of putting the patrol in for a commendation. I don't know where they really went or what they saw, but a few hours later I found out that the intelligence section, when reading the aerial photo of Group Lorraine, had the picture upside down. When read properly it showed there was a twenty-foot ditch, thirty feet wide, with the bottom of it filled with coiled barbed wire and mines.

We tried again in the afternoon to move forward to where we could shoot at them, but the number of wounded and killed increased under the heavy fire.

Late in the evening I was ordered to come back to battalion for further orders. It had rained all day and most of the night, and the path down the hill was a mud "Lob Lolly" because of the support people bringing supplies up and taking wounded out. I stopped to let Lieutenant Phyffer know where I was going. An 88mm shell hit in a tree about thirty feet high and to our left; it killed one man close by and wounded another. A piece of shrapnel caught Lieutenant Phyffer's field jacket at the right shoulder and cut it down to his left hip. Once again he lost a set of clothes, but never lost a drop of blood. We were both deaf in the ear that had been facing that shell burst for three or four days.

After this shell exploded I went back to battalion to see what was being cooked up for the next day. The path was so slippery that I fell down. I got up, slipped down again. So I just sat down in the mud, sitting on one foot with the other foot out in front, and slid down the hill. When I slowed down I pulled myself along by the bushes and small trees on each side of the path. I finally got down with a lap full of mud. Why stay on the path at all? Well, there had been enough people on that path to know there were no mines.

When the Company Commanders assembled at Battalion Headquarters we were told that we would be relieved the next day. With the news that there was no wall, but a dry moat into which the Germans could fire into our ranks, it was decided we would leave Group Lorraine alone and approach Metz another way.

I went back to the company and passed the word that we would be relieved. I spent one more night in the hollow that I had dug. I was a little frightened of sleeping in it because, with rain and shells exploding, it kept caving in—so I slept what time I slept outside of that hole.

We were supposed to have forty-man platoons. These were the numbers that we had for Killed In Action, Seriously Wounded, and Unfit after the third day on the 1st Sergeant's strength report:

First Platoon	*19 present*	*KIA—2, SWA—4, UF—2*
Second Platoon	*20 present*	*KIA—1, SWA—3, UF—4*
Third Platoon	*25 present*	
Fourth Platoon	*28 present*	*KIA—1, UF—1*
	92	

I never did see a forty-man platoon.

It was nice to be getting out of the line for a little while. But the company that relieved us was surrounded before we reached the rest area, and C Company was ordered to go back and run the Germans out from behind the company that had taken our place. Our luck held out; by the time C Company got turned around and had started back, a runner came down from Battalion to say the situation was under control, and we could go back to the rest area.

We walked back and had the company tied in before dark. It seemed so peaceful and quiet. The last time I had seen my sleeping bag was the night of September 8, when I arrived at Division Rear twenty miles from the front lines. How long C

Company had gone without a rest I didn't know. I had only been with them for eleven days by then.

When I finally decided to go to sleep, I pitched my pup tent, took off my wet muddy clothes all the way to my birthday suit, and slid into my sleeping bag. I put my rifle on my left side, laid my pistol on my stomach, and went to sleep—some sleep, anyway. I awoke only once. Our field telephone had been put close to me. Sometime during the night the guard on the phone was changed and the new guard moved in my direction without a helmet on. My pistol came up as he squatted down by the phone. He never knew how close he came to being shot by his own Company Commander.

Below: American soldiers fight 300 yards from the front line. (Hulton-Deutsch Collection / Corbis)

It had been rumored that General Patton had said that the 3rd Army would take Metz even if it took a $2\frac{1}{2}$-ton truck full of dog tags to do it. It would have for sure, if we had to capture Metz with head-on attacks against the forts.

The next day we began to move again. We were not going back in against Metz. We were taking another position in the line. It was quiet. We were to occupy a defensive position close to a town called Piervillers, a village to the northwest of Metz. I was to have a room in one of the village houses still occupied by its owners. It was one of those houses that you read about—the cow and calf and the pigs live in the basement and the family live upstairs.

When we first moved into this new area, we didn't know what to expect. One of the first questions that comes to mind when an outfit goes into a defensive position is, What is the possibility of an attack? Where would we be attacked? How long will it be before we can expect an attack? C Company was on the left flank of the regiment. The boundary on our left was a road that led right into Metz. The terrain in front of us was fairly level—level enough for tanks. To the right and front the terrain turned hilly. In Louisiana it would be called mountains. We were in positions close enough to the hills so that Group Lorraine's guns couldn't fire on us.

We began to plan the defensive position. First we surveyed the terrain to see where and how we could best use our automatic weapons for covering fire—where to put the machine guns, where to put the riflemen to protect the machine guns and to cover the front of the position, where to put the 60mm mortars so they could fire on places forward of our position that could not be covered by machine-gun fire, and to cover the whole front if necessary. This was all worked out on paper ahead of time.

The rumor came down we should dig in deep, because we might be there through the winter. We dug, we checked to see that the foxholes in the line were deep enough and covered over well enough. I dug a foxhole for myself and put straw in the bottom of it and checked it out by sitting in it. So there I was sitting looking up, and I discovered I was under an apple tree. The apples were just turning red. I exploded out of that foxhole, up that apple tree, grabbed two apples, and was back in my foxhole. They were the first whole apples I had seen in two years. The area was a pear and apple orchard. The local people must have noticed that we were eating their fruit. They began a quick pick to save their crop from fruit-hungry Americans.

As days came and went, we became more relaxed. No shells had come in; no reports of German tanks came down. We knew there were Germans out there somewhere, because two of them decided they had had enough war and came over and surrendered to us. I began to worry about snipers. I could never find myself any olive drab long drawers—I only had white ones. It made me rather nervous to pull my pants down and show that white underwear. I could imagine a sniper aiming at my exposed drawers.

We were able to pull a few men out of the line to go back to a bathhouse not too far from the front to get a bath and clean clothes. My gear with my change of clothes had come up, so I was very happy when my turn for a bath came. I hadn't had one since I had left England on August 9.

■　■　■

Our Blood and His Guts

*I*n planning the defense of our Regimental Area it turned out that in front of my company was the only tank approach on the regimental front. Immediately, the 90th Division engineers were in my area laying mines. Not having seen a German tank yet, except the burnt-out hulls I saw when travelling across France, and not really having any desire to see one coming at me, I felt a little more safe behind all those mines.

During our reconnaissance, one of the things that made me a little nervous in the service was the German Tellermine. It is large, about thirteen inches in diameter, about $2\frac{1}{2}$ inches thick, and it is filled with explosives. The firing device is in a hole right in the middle, and it could be set with side and bottom triggers, too, to dissuade tampering. We were picked up by a jeep to meet the Battalion Commander at an observation post on a hill back behind our position. There was an anti-aircraft gun on this hill. People had collected some of these Tellermines and they used them in their defense, digging holes in the gravel roads to plant them. On our way up to the observation post I looked down just in time to see the jeep wheel roll over a mine.

I broke out in sweat all over, and I talked real unfriendly to that driver. Fortunately, it takes the weight of a tank to activate that type of mine, and the jeep wouldn't set it off. But—just the same!

We were nearly dug in. We had been working on it for about a week when word came down that all officers would report to Battalion. We wondered what this was about. We were loaded on trucks. Where we went I don't know. We were served a very nice steak dinner, had a beer or two. After dinner I ran into General Weaver and had a few words with him. He asked how I was getting along. Considering all things, I told him all right so far.

When I got back to my seat, the group grew quiet. The stage—I didn't realize until then we were in a shot-up theater— lit up. Out from the wings came the Commanding General of the 3rd Army, General Patton. He walked out on stage with everything shining—his boots, his buttons, his ivory-handled .45s, and especially those three stars on his helmet.

He started his address to us by saying: "I came here to tell you sons-of-bitches how to fight, but I can't do that because you are already fighting a bunch of sons-of-bitches." Somewhere in his speech he said, "I don't want anybody in my command to die for his country. I want you to make those other sons-of-bitches die for their country." Thoughts on the General were pro and con, but the regular infantryman would rather tell you that he was in the 3rd Army with General Patton than in any other part of the war. General Patton was called "Old Blood and Guts," and if you listened a little longer after you heard that, you would also hear, "Yes, our blood and his guts."

This was the first get-together of the 90th Division officers that I had been in on, and I never experienced another.

■ ■ ■

I inspected positions and weapons, moved around trying to meet the noncommissioned officers. I didn't want to know them as well as I did my noncoms in the company that I left in England. It hurts too much to watch friends become Killed In Action and Wounded In Action.

Replacements were beginning to trickle in. I soon had enough officers to fill the company—not enough enlisted replacements, but some. General Patton had broken out of the beachhead and captured Brest (a big seaport we needed badly) then turned and ran across France and captured Paris and started toward Germany. After that, the powers that be were sure the war was nearly over in Europe. The replacements were turned around to go to the Pacific War.

Then, as our forces reached the edge of Germany, the Germans pulled men and units from somewhere and everywhere. Instead of being able to run across the countryside, we had to fight our way for every foot. In addition to the replacement problems, there was this interservice thing. General Montgomery of the UK had sold the British on an operation that we know as "The Bridge Too Far." There was just one problem—this operation of Montgomery's to the north needed most of the supplies that General Patton also needed to keep the pressure on the Germans.

High Command decided that General Montgomery's operation would shorten the war. Well, it caused the war to last longer because the operation failed. The paratroopers were dropped and they did a good job, but the ground forces that were supposed to link up with the paratroopers did not get there. The German forces in front of General Patton became stronger, more organized, and harder to dig out of their positions.

■ ■ ■

We were beginning to feel at home. We had been in our defensive position for three weeks. The only action we had was when a German patrol waylaid one of our motorized patrols and killed or captured all except the Sergeant Patrol Leader. He was one of my platoon leaders, and they had tried to make an officer out of him many times—a battlefield commission. When the German patrol started shooting, he peeled out of that jeep and through the woods until he got back to our position.

Soon after this happened, word came down that we were going to move in position for an attack on Maizieres-les-Metz. It was the next town before Piervillers, and was a steel mill town. We had taken the steel mill, but we didn't have the slag pile, nor the town. So we started making preparations to leave; the first thing that had to be done was to pick up all of those tank mines that had been put down in front of my company. It was necessary for the engineers to come in and dig them up, and put the safety device back on them to make them safe to move.

A jeep with a trailer sat in the middle of the company, and the engineers were loading mines. Six engineers were standing around the half-full trailer when one of them dropped a mine. The mine must have had a defective firing device—it exploded. All the mines exploded. They blew a hole in the ground big enough to drop a $2\frac{1}{2}$-ton truck into.

A dog ran through the area later on; I saw him pick up a string of flesh. This was the only evidence that there had been six men there. The explosion blackened the ground and blew the leaves off the fruit trees for fifty yards. We never found any part of the trailer, very little of the jeep. We never knew whether it was a careless accident—not putting the safety ring in the right place—or whether it was actually a bad firing device. All of the witnesses went with the explosion.

■ ■ ■

We moved to our next position, getting set up for the next attack. We still had a big gap in our line. The Free French Forces showed up armed with U.S. equipment. I don't know where they came from, how they got there, but there they were. They were allowed to move into the gap. It started raining, and the early mornings started getting cold. After about ten days the Free French Forces went walking back out of the gap and left our flank wide open. I do not know what the problem was with these units.

The night the French left, it got so quiet I guess the German unit in front of us decided to find out what we were doing and where we were doing it. The Germans sent a combat patrol in our direction, and they got right into the middle of our company. All of a sudden there were German machine pistols shooting all around. One of our machine guns opened up, hand grenades started going off. Most everybody in the company was keeping in their foxholes to let the German patrol move around and get out without finding what size unit we had. The shooting and explosions died down, and everything got quiet again.

Above: Infantrymen, one with a top hat picked up in a nearby town, sit on a disabled German vehicle resting on the rim of the crater made by a bomb. (FDR Library)

I talked to the platoon leaders. They hadn't lost anybody. The Germans must have gotten out because no dead at all were reported. But they sure threw some lead around. The next morning there were two fresh bullet holes in a tree right above where I was lying in a slit trench.

The day came for the attack and in went C Company. There were Germans dug in around the top of the slag pile. All our rifle platoon leaders were wounded along with a number of our

noncoms. Capturing the town of Maizieres-les-Metz was difficult because it was well defended, and it took days to get the
Germans out. The town had antipersonnel mines all over the
place. It was the first time I had seen concrete mines. They were
stuck in the ground on the end of sticks. When they were set off,
the concrete was blown in every directions.

When it came fighting, I was cautious. You fired your 8-
round rifle five times, which was all the rounds the German
guns fired, then you waited for the other man to show his head,
thinking you were out of ammunition. The carbines we officers
were given didn't work as well. I shot at one man four times, but
he just got up and ran away.

I said I was cautious. As for feeling any fear—I was scared
all the time.

It was a very difficult fight. When on top of the slag pile, the
men were exposed to rifle and machine-gun fire from below, in
addition to the artillery fire coming from two directions. Two
men did their part before one was killed and one badly
wounded. One had two pistols that he had been keeping, one
German P-38, one American .45 automatic. When he reached
the top of the slag pile, he took his pistols, one in each hand, and
started running around the top edge of the slag pile shooting
the Germans dug in just below the crest. How many he killed I
don't know, but at the opposite end of the pile a German sniper
in the town killed him. The second man was a Sergeant who had
been in so long that he didn't believe anything could happen to
him. He was standing on the forward edge of the slag pile
directing mortar fire over a radio, and he took a German bullet
through the chest.

But the first WIA on this attack was a new Lieutenant,
another one whose name I never knew. He led in the 1st Platoon, and in the dark a German machine gun opened up on
them. He was wounded badly. A Sergeant right behind him was
carrying a hand grenade in his hand with the pin already out
and threw it into the machine-gun nest. He killed all but the
machine gunner. The gunner jumped up and hollered "*Kamerad.*" They took him prisoner.

They brought the wounded Lieutenant back past where I was, along with the prisoner. He was carrying one end of the Lieutenant's litter. They told me how the prisoner had wounded the Lieutenant and then jumped up and surrendered. It made me so mad my rifle was pointing in the prisoner's middle before I could stop it. I could have shot him and danced on his remains. But the thought came to me that it was just not right. I couldn't kill him in cold blood. He had no harm left in him.

■　■　■

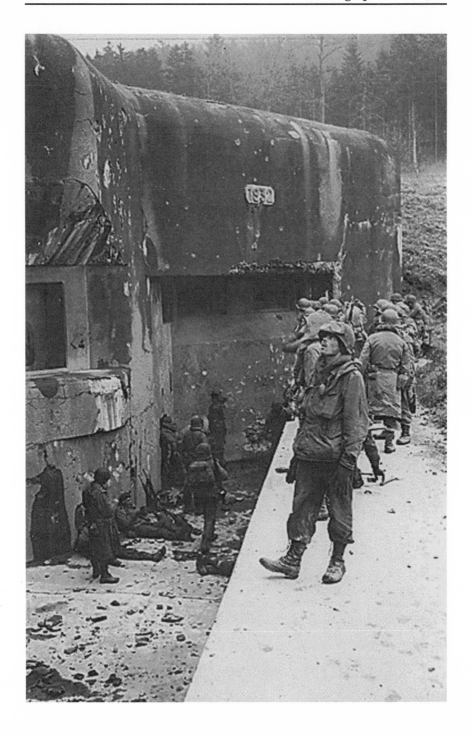

Across the Maginot Line

The word came that General Weaver's former aide, the one who had suffered a stomach wound, would not be sent back to the front. I was ordered to Division Headquarters. I was back to Maizieres-les-Metz the next day, this time as General Weaver's Section Chief. I could not be General Weaver's aide because he was a one-star general and was only allowed a Lieutenant for an aide. I was a Captain; so, until General Weaver was promoted to a two-star General, I would be a Section Chief.

My first sergeant and the Company Commander who took over C Company were killed by the same 88mm shell, not too long after I left to join General Weaver's staff.

The General, as Assistant Division Commander, was supposed to meet with Regimental and Battalion Commanders during time of attack to see how the operations were going. However, catching up with these commanders, who were usually forward where they could see what was going on in the companies and platoons, usually made a person wish he had something to hide behind.

This was the first time that I had seen any psychological warfare. We were still trying to get the Germans out of Maizieres-les-Metz. Metz had not been captured by any army in fifteen hundred years, and fighting was fierce—house to house, floor to floor, room to room. The Germans had made a two-story stone building in the middle of town a strongpoint, and we couldn't get them out. Some garages backed up to the railroad track, and the back end of the garages pointed toward the strongpoint. We backed a halftrack with big speakers into one of those garages, and a self-propelled 155mm gun was driven into the second garage. For a while the psychological warfare people would talk to the Germans about how nice they would be treated if they surrendered. If nothing happened, and no one gave up, then they would let the 155mm gun talk for a while. I don't know which worked, but Maizieres-les-Metz was ours the next day, the 30th of October.

Things had changed; people had changed. I no longer had the responsibility of running a company. I just had the responsibility of getting done what the General wanted done. It was not always in the form of an order. The General suggested and I complied. The General would say, "We are going to see what Colonel Bacon's Regiment is doing tomorrow." It would then be my job to find out everything I could about Colonel Bacon, because I didn't know Colonel Bacon from Adam.

I would first go to the G-1 section (Personnel) to get a little background information. Then to the G-2 section (Intelligence) and there find out as much as possible about the Germans that were facing Colonel Bacon's regiment, the 359th. Go then to the G-3 section (Plans and Operations) to find out what the regiment was supposed to be doing and when the regiment would move on the plans. G-4 would be last (Supply) just to keep contact with our supply, which is big business. Of course, I did not pick this up right away. There is no handbook as to what one is supposed to do as a General's Section Chief. Like most jobs, it took time to learn and to perform.

I had very few people to work with—the General; the driver, Perko; and the General's striker–batman–man's man–orderly, Garman. Garman saw to it that the General had fresh clothes no matter where we were. I never knew how he did this. Garman was more like a son to the General. He tried to keep the General in good humor, making jokes in his heavy Brooklyn accent. Perko drove the jeep with the General's stars on it. Perko was a talented driver—he handled a jeep like no other driver I ever saw. He handled a rifle as well as he handled a jeep and always ready to grab his weapon when he thought the General was in danger. It was up to me to see to it that we didn't get killed, because I was the one who had to read the maps and know where all the headquarters were. It was not very hard, riding around in the front lines, to end up on a road on which the Germans had observation. They really had a good time when they caught a jeep running down a road that they could shoot at. We called those roads 88 Boulevards.

Shortly after I became General Weaver's Section Chief, the 90th Division was ordered out of the front lines for a ten-day R&R&T—Rest, Recuperation, and Training. We eased out of the lines to Mercy le Bas, far enough back so that we could train ten hours a day for a sneak crossing of the Moselle River.

When I said *we* when I was Company Commander of C Company 357th Infantry, I was referring to about one hundred ninety men. Now that I belonged to the personal staff of a two-star Major General who was the Assistant Division Commander ACG—the Assistant Commanding General—*we* meant a division of about 20,000 men.

In this sneak river crossing it was necessary for the 90th Division to "disappear." As we began our move to the rest/training area, all of the truck markings had to be covered up. Dust clouds had to be made in the rear of the lines in the direction that we were not going, hopefully confusing the Germans as to what we were up to.

There was no reason not to believe that there would be more people like the woman at Hayange trying to tell the Germans about our movements. When they don't get caught they are, I guess, just local people with radios. When they get caught they are spies.

There were many people in France who figured the Germans had been there long enough. Many wanted them out. Many wanted them in, and lots of those who wanted them in didn't mind telling the Krauts what units were in their towns, which directions the gas trucks, ammunition trucks, trucks carrying troops, trucks pulling artillery pieces were going. These are just bits and pieces of information, but as this information comes in, it begins to build a full picture. We were doing everything possible to block information on our move from the lines, our ten days of refitting, retraining, getting replacements.

The training for the river crossing was very difficult. The boats would have to be hand-carried nearly a thousand yards before they got to the Moselle River. It had to be done quietly. The General was running from one place to another to see how things were progressing, but he was interested in more than the training. The General staff (G-1, G-2, G-3, G-4) met every day. The G-1 (Personnel) would give his report on the number of replacements (officers and enlisted men) who had come up and what units they had been assigned to. The G-2 (Intelligence Officer) would report on what we had done to keep from giving away our position. He would also report on what was new on the German side of the lines. G-2 got his information from higher Headquarters, divisions on each side of us, aerial photos, the amount of artillery the Germans were firing. We had little spotter airplanes up each day, which were used to direct artillery fire and to report what they saw.

The G-3 (Plans and Training Officer) reported on the progress of the plan for the river crossing: who would make the crossing, how many boats would go in the first wave, how the boats would get back across the river, how the boat crews would find their way to the river in the dark, how many men in each boat, what weapons go across first, where the supporting weapons are set up to cover the crossing, what are the dividing lines between regiments, what are the objectives for each regiment on crossing the river. And a hundred or more other questions that had to be answered.

G-4 (Supply) would report on our fuel tonnage, ammunition tonnage, the chances of baths for the men, when there would be a new ration of clothes (it was beginning to get cold at night), and how transportation was holding up.

It had in fact been getting cold before I left C Company. We got one ration of clothes while I was there. I didn't exchange anything. I just took a larger size that I could pull over what I already had on. Baggy, but good insulation.

The buildup for the river crossing was coming along fine. The Engineering Commander met with the Division Staff and reported the floating bridge equipment was behind us under cover, in position to come forward and start bridging after the assault units had gotten across the Moselle.

The chosen spot was near Cattenom and Kerling. This was where the great French defensive line, the Maginot line, crossed the Moselle River. The French had thought for a long time that they were safe from invasion. Some of the Maginot defensive line descended seven stories underground. The Maginot Line was supposed to warn against surprise attacks, but it didn't help the French very much when the Germans attacked. The Germans just ran around the end through Belgium and came in the back door.

I spent a good bit of time visiting along the line, because there were observation posts that we could climb into and look over the Moselle River. The more one knows about where one is going, the easier it is to get there. One of the things I saw that I didn't like very much was a fort on the German side, Fort Koenigsmacher. Fort Koenigsmacher protected the northern approaches to Metz and was located close to the southern side of the Maginot Line, just east of the Moselle. Fort Koenigsmacher was ominous looking. It had what looked like a turtle shell on top of it with an artillery piece sticking out of the turtle's back. I hadn't seen the top of Group Lorraine—the fort that my old Battalion attacked. We never got as close.

Early morning on the day for the crossing, November 9, the infantry went forward with the assault boats, following the ribbons and ropes that had been laid out during the night to keep the boat leaders from losing their way. Two battalions went across the river so quietly that not a single shot was fired. The first battalion began to clean out the little town of Koenigsmacher. The other battalions of the regiments began to make their way forward across the Moselle. The combat engineers were right behind to put two floating bridges across the river— one at Cattenom and one at Malling. They were doing a wonderful job of getting them across, but something woke up the enemy. The Germans flooded the valley by releasing water from a dam somewhere. The Moselle began to rise so fast that it washed out both bridges. The engineers caught the floating bridges and anchored them until they could be put back in place.

The second day we needed the bridges even more. There were wounded men on the opposite bank to take back to the hospitals. Up until then the only medical help was the first-aid men who moved with the infantry. Ammunition and food had to be supplied. More troops had to get across to support the troops already there.

The bridges were nearly in place, but this time the Germans shot them out. The engineers worked during the night and managed to get the bridge at Malling in place. The third day, the Germans mounted an early morning counterattack.

The Germans had quickly set up tanks and infantry to kick us back into the river. Their infantry may have been as large as a small battalion—maybe 300 soldiers. They were walking, trotting, and following the half-dozen tanks. Because of tank support, our tank destroyer units were to go across first. Tank destroyers looked something like a tank, but were open at the top and were armed with our 90mm antitank gun, the only gun that could stand up in a fight with a German "Tiger tank."

Our forward observers began to call for fire support. There were sixteen battalions of artillery set up to support the river crossing, and they were just waiting for someone to holler for help. The 105s, 155s, 8-inch guns were all set to go. The FO's called for "Time on Targets" in the area where the counterattack was coming in; one hundred ninety-two pieces of artillery began to fire on the German counterattack. In addition, the infantry the Germans were attacking opened up with rifle and machine-gun fire. Another company to the left of the attack that the Germans hadn't seen wheeled and began to fire rifles, machine guns, and mortars into the German right flank.

Three of our tank destroyers from the 773rd TD Battalion rolled up on shore as the German tanks came into view. The tank destroyers knocked out four of the tanks, and the other two surrendered. The fire had the area so completely covered, I cannot see how any of the Germans in the counterattack got out alive besides the two tank crews.

The fourth tank destroyer went down in the middle of the river. The Germans had shot out the bridge again.

The General decided that some moral support should be moved across the river. One "duck" (the DUKW, a $2\frac{1}{2}$-ton truck fitted for amphibious operation) tried to get across at Cattenom, but there was a minefield along the edge of the bank, covered by

Above: The Third Army crosses the Moselle River in assault craft. (Corbis / Bettmann)

water at this high tide, and the DUKW blew up, killing the driver. The duck had been loaded with supplies, and I don't know how many other men were killed.

The General watched this, then said to me and Garman, "Let's cross." A motorboat was produced from somewhere; when we got to the far side and the boat hit the bank, I expected to be blown sky high. Nothing happened. I jumped out of the boat to hold it still for the General to get out. I knew we were in the minefield; I wondered when I would step on one of the mines. We walked out of that water without blowing ourselves up. From then on, those paratroop boots I had on were my lucky boots.

There were no medical facilities on the east side of the Moselle River except for company-aid men, and they soon ran out of supplies. One of our little artillery spotter planes dropped supplies wrapped in blankets. The blankets helped to keep some of the supplies from being destroyed in the drop, but weren't too effective. A first aid station was set up in one house, and General Weaver, Garman, and I took over another for his forward headquarters until we could do better.

The combat engineers worked another night, and this time a bridge stayed in, and everything needed to sustain the troops already across the Moselle River came forward: more troops, tanks, tank destroyers, supplies, and aid stations.

The fresh troops that came across spread out southeast and east. Things quieted down close to the river. Fort Koenigsmacher was only a short distance to the south from the town. On the fifth and sixth days, our artillery rained on the fort so heavily that the German commanding officer let his men come into the fort. This was a mistake. There was no one on the outside to protect the fort and there were not enough firing slits in the walls for the soldiers inside to protect either it or themselves.

Below: A US tank destroyer crosses a stream marking the German border near Hammeres, Germany. In the background is a destroyed German railroad bridge. September 12, 1944. (US Army Military History Institute)

At this point it came down to, How do we get the turtle out of his shell? There were very few doors on the fort, and those doors had firing ports on them. There had to be ventilators with pipes coming out of the side or roofs somewhere. Our troops found them and started dropping hand grenades down the pipes. They poured gasoline down the ventilators, dropped hand grenades, and they threw satchel charges against the doors. Along about noon the three hundred German officers and soldiers decided to save themselves for the next war and came marching out of the fort.

Fort Koenigsmacher was the first fort to surrender in the Metz defences.

The fort descended four or five stories underground. It was the only place that I took a souvenir. The Germans had what we called a "burp gun," or Schmeisser machine pistol. It was the personal weapon of many of their infantry soldiers. It was somewhat like an American submachine gun, but better. It fired 9mm ammunition twice as fast as anything we had. Without thinking, I reached down to where it was lying in a pile of rifles on the floor and picked one up. Luckily, it wasn't booby-trapped.

It was the fourth day after the capture of Fort Koenigsmacher that the bridge at Malling finally stayed in. Then there was the big push to get everything across the river that was needed across. None of the artillery had to be moved yet, because it had been put in position to cover the objectives of the regiments with both supporting and defensive fire. Perko got across the bridge with the jeep, which the General was very happy about. He liked the infantry, but he didn't like walking.

■ ■ ■

Top Brass

This whole river crossing was about capturing Metz, a large town on the German border. Instead of trying to capture the forts that protected Metz, which would have killed thousands of troops, the 3rd Army Headquarters commanded by General Patton decided to do it right—which was to cross the Moselle River south of Metz and north of Metz, go into Germany behind Metz, and cut all the roads leading in or out. When they had run out of gasoline, ammunition and food, the Germans would likely surrender the city.

After the bridge at Malling stayed in, the 359th Regiment was able to push on to their objective. The 357th (my old Regiment) straddled the Maginot Line, and the Germans were using some of the forts on the line very well. They had some machine guns mounted on elevated pedestals. When they were down you couldn't see them, and you could walk right over them. My former Battalion Commander, Colonel George B. Barth, went by one of those "pop up" machine-gun nests and they shot him in the backside. I saw him as he was evacuated on a litter. His wound was serious and he never made it back to the front.

We were real proud of Fort Koenigsmacher, because our third regiment (the 358th) had captured it, and that was the first and last fort captured by assault. The word got around and we had a parade of top brass come to see.

■ ■ ■

General Weaver, Perko, Garman, and I were waiting around getting ready to go somewhere, and I noticed General Weaver moving around excitedly. I looked and there was one of those big six-wheeled armored scout cars coming up. As it got fairly close to where we were, it stopped, and two officers stood up in the front and began to wave and shout, "Hey, Bill! Hey, Bill!" They were, of course, addressing General Weaver. The General came to attention in his best West Point style and saluted. I saw that one of the officers standing up had two stars on his helmet. This was Major General Johnny Walker, the 20th Corps Commander which was the corps the 90th Divisions was in. The other had three stars—this was 3rd Army Commander Lieutenant General George Patton. The rest of us saluted also.

After they had talked a minute, General Weaver said, "General Patton, I want you to meet my new aide, Captain Mayhall."

I was standing at my best attention and still saluting. General Patton turned to me, and I felt that he was looking right down through me to my heels. Then he said, "Mayhall, you got your Goddamn work cut out for you."

I only knew General Weaver at that time as a fighting general, a good boss, and a very considerate man to be around. It was later that I began to understand what General Patton might have been talking about. General Weaver didn't like to stay still. He hated the Germans from the first World War. He liked to wander around where the action was going on. He liked to see how the soldiers were making out. On the personal side, he liked to drink not a little bit but a whole lot. On one of his first assignments after graduation from West Point, Class of 1912, he was a 2nd Lieutenant commanding a platoon on the Mexican border. He overdrank and had his platoon across the Mexican border, and nearly caused an international incident. Of course he was sent before some kind of board, and he stayed a Lieutenant for a long time.

He was in the infantry in WWI. He was wounded, and before he got well and while his stitches were still in, Patton, Walker, and one or more of his buddies found a wheelchair, lifted Weaver out of one of the windows, and rolled him off to one of the local bars. When they finally decided to call it a

Above: Lt. Glenn Alliger and Pvt. Bernard Schmidt pause to look at a WWI memorial to the Third Division at Chateau Thierry, France, which has been left in ruins by retreating Germans. (US Army Military History Institute)

night, they rolled Weaver up the hill toward the hospital, and at the top of the hill a big discussion on some matter came up. In the heated argument they forgot about the wheelchair and Weaver rolled downhill, picking up speed as he went. The wheelchair turned a couple of flips and threw the Lieutenant out, tumbled him around very hard. His buddies finally went into pursuit. When they caught up with him, he had popped his stitches and was bleeding all over the place. They carried him up to the hospital and straight to the operating room to get his stitches put back in. So we can determine that the old Generals of World War II were the tough but playful young officers of World War I.

■ ■ ■

The General told me to get Perko and go back to Division Headquarters and pick up Lieutenant somebody. It was a terrible night to be out. It was raining. It was dark. The only light by which to see the road was flashes of artillery fire. General Lee had a Lieutenant on his staff whom he sent around to take care of the generals. This Lieutenant was an orthopedic doctor. His job was to put our generals on a table and pop their back bones, rub their muscles to take away some of their tension and strain. Perko and I found the Lieutenant and brought him back across the Moselle River to Koenigsmacher.

He didn't like the rain, the dark, or the flashes of artillery fire. This was the first time he had been this far forward. The next morning he gave the General a good workout, and the general said it helped a lot. The doctor went to work on me, but he just seemed to be tickling me. I laughed so much he had to quit.

Below: Overturned tank by a Belgian bridge. (FDR Library)

The General invited the Lieutenant to stay with us a few more days, but the Lieutenant said he had a lot more Generals to go see. But to me he said, "Get me the hell out of this place. That cannon fire makes me nervous."

The next day the General wanted to see what had gone on during the counterattack from Kerling. We drove into the battlefield where, because of the difficulty in crossing the river and in accomplishing the assigned objectives, the field had not been cleaned up. By that I mean the dead were still there. The burned-out German tanks were there, and the big surprise to me was the number of unexploded shells. It made me wonder if the artillery shells were being made so fast that the factories were not getting them right—or whether they were being deliberately sabotaged.

Then we drove south along the river to see Colonel Bacon, who was now in the 95th Division and was running a task force close to the Moselle straight into the north of Metz. His task force had crossed the Moselle at Thionville.

We went into one little town along the river that really made our hair stand on end. We drove into the town square and stopped. Perko turned off the motor. The General began to look around. The windows to the houses were open; the white curtains were blowing in the wind. Not a sound. Perko, Garman, and I all reached back into the jeep and grabbed our rifles. We were afraid we had rolled into something. We were going to have to shoot our way out. Nothing happened. No noise. No movement. Everyone had run off somewhere and hidden. It was spooky to be in a village with no noises of any kind.

Back to the General's Headquarters in Koenigsmacher. The General got a message from Division Headquarters that a Lieutenant he had been looking for had arrived. The General told me to go get this next Lieutenant Somebody without telling me who he was. When I got to Division, I found a tall lanky, young man looking around like he had maybe done the wrong thing coming there. It was the General's son, 1st Lieutenant William G. Weaver, Jr. I was soon calling him "Bill," and I liked him right away. He had been having trouble getting overseas. He had gone through OCS, got his commission, then went through paratrooper school where they made him an instructor. Then he went through tank school, where they also made him an instructor. I think maybe the General's wife was keeping him out of harm's way. Finally he wrote his father and asked him to get him overseas. He expected to go to West Point eventually, and combat on his record would look good.

We got back to Koenigsmacher and took Bill to see his father. Garman had set him up a place to sleep. In the meantime the Germans were trying to keep the 90th Division from cutting off the roads into the east side of Metz. One battalion of the 358th Infantry Regiment had captured the little town of Distroff. This was the most threatening to the Germans, so the Germans counterattacked in regimental strength. It was late in the evening. The Germans attacked with tanks and infantry. It was so fast that it couldn't be stopped before they had broken into the Battalion area and captured and taken prisoner the Battalion Commander. The forward observers for the mortar companies, for the artillery, got on their radios and telephones and started calling for those sixteen battalions of artillery. They began to fire. They had a fire plan that boxed in Distroff. The infantry riflemen and machine-gunners were already fighting for their lives. The concentrated fire of all those weapons soon broke the counterattack.

The next morning the General said, "Let's go see." We took off for Distroff and parked the jeep behind a building. The ground fighting had stopped, but the artillery had only slowed down. We had made the mistake of taking Bill with us, and he was having trouble. After being in the front lines for a while, one learns which artillery shells are coming in and which ones are going out. Poor young Bill—he was ducking both ours and the enemy's. It was terrifying to him. One shell came right over the building we were walking behind and burst on the building across the street. We all ducked and dropped to the ground. We got up and looked for Bill. In ducking he had reinjured his knees, which he had injured in paratroop school—off to the hospital with him.

We went on. The General had to reestablish the battalion staff so that it could function again. I walked up to a tank destroyer behind a building and looked around it. There were two big holes in the front of the TD. They were so close together they formed a figure eight. I got the story of how it was knocked out. The action took place after dark. The TD crew heard this German tank rumbling around in the dark. The noise sounded so close and so loud that they fired a couple of rounds at where they thought the German tank was, but they missed. It must have been very frightening to the German tankers; the muzzle blast of a 90mm cannon is terrible. The German tankers didn't like being shot at, so they shot up a flare, which lighted the whole area. They fired two rounds into our TD and knocked it out. I know there were many more TDs knocked out, but that was the only one I saw before they could get the dead out of it.

The General went into the Battalion Headquarters, and I went on walking around. I reached the edge of the village that the regimental attack had come from. There were dead Krauts all over the place. Over an area greater than two football fields men lay in every position there was. Not ten yards square without at least two Germans. All were dead—except for one.

Out in the middle of this field of death, I could see the arm of one badly wounded German come up very slowly and go back down. At the time I was mad enough to think it was a pretty sight. It meant one less of them to kill our soldiers. If someone were to ask me whether I'd killed any Germans, I would have gladly told them, Every damned one I could.

This again was the effect of massed artillery. The Germans thought we had a new weapon, automatic artillery—sixteen Battalions of Artillery can put so many shells on a counterattack. If not for our artillery, the German Regimental attack would have completely wiped out our position.

■ ■ ■

The division was on its objective, which was to close with other divisions coming from the south and to cut all roads going in and out of Metz. Upon completion of this operation, the 90th Infantry Division was to attack to the east, forcing a crossing of

Above: Two American soldiers look down on a long row of "dragon's teeth" concrete devices devised to halt invading Allied tanks at the Siegfried Line. September 15, 1944. (National Archives Central Plains Region)

the Saar River. The division crossed the river, where it stayed bogged down. I'm glad that I wasn't there.

I was glad that I was not there because the 90th Division crossed the Saar River and then ran into the prepared concrete positions of the Siegfried Line. The heavy, desperate fighting did not get the 90th through the built-up defensive position.

What about Metz? Other troops were moving ever closer to it. The 90th Division battled their way on down to where they linked up with the 5th Division coming up from the south. This completed the surrounding of Metz. We cut off supplies going in so that, after a while, the townspeople and soldiers noticed that food, ammunition, and gasoline were getting short. The civilians welcomed the American soldiers into town, and the German soldiers held up their hands, surrendered, and asked for a trip to the States. Somehow it had never occurred to me that some of the thousands of German soldiers who were captured were going to the United States.

The town was taken. Some of the forts around Metz surrendered, but Group Lorraine—the fort my battalion was trying to capture—never surrendered until after peace was declared.

■ ■ ■

GI's have you ever figured it out?

70 American men out of a hundred are enjoying peace in civil life; 22 are training and stationed back home; 8 are doing their bit overseas —

4 men out of a hundred are engaged in actual fighting.

Some 60 divisions have reached the fronts; combat troops as well as service units, totalling more than 2 155 000 officers and men accompanied these divisions abroad.

Adding the million men of the Air Forces, there is a total of 3 055 000 GI's on the world's battle fronts.

(Stars and Stripes, Sept 20, page 4)

And only about half of these are doing the grim, nasty job of actual fighting.

Almost every day you front-line men read of people at home leaving war jobs for something more secure which will carry them trough the post-war period.

For you the advice of these people is.

Keep soldiers in the Army after the war till jobs can be secured for them.

The draft-dodgers at home expect every Joe to do his duty!

Opposite: German propaganda leaflet.

The Hurtgen Forest

*I*t was now was between the 15th and 25th of November 1944. General McLain, our wonderful Division Commander all the way across France, had been promoted to a three-star General and given the 19th Corps. The 90th Infantry Division was to be commanded by a new general by the name of Van Fleet. General Weaver outranked General Van Fleet, so higher headquarters had to find another place for General Weaver. He was promoted and ordered to take over as Commanding General of the 8th Infantry Division now in action in the Hurtgen Forest. General Gerow, who had been C.O. of the 8th Division, was being sent back to the States.

This was a big blow to General Weaver. He had learned to love and respect the officers and men of the 90th Division; he liked the sound of the "Texas-Oklahoma Tough 'Ombres." The 8th Division had come out of its rest area where the Germans would mount their big drive, the Bulge. When General Weaver took command of the 8th Division, it was struggling with the worst terrain, the worst kind of weather, and very unfriendly Germans.

General Weaver told us—me, Perko, Garman—to prepare for the move so that we would be ready for change of command on November 28. We were going a good distance to the north. We didn't have too much time to think about General Weaver's Packard, with all the disturbance of promotions and changes of command, but with the Division breaking into Germany, the General would need his car for his ride down the main drag in Berlin. The General had to see some people on his way, so the first stop was in Luxembourg where the General commanding the 1st Army had his headquarters. General Weaver had to report to, and I got to meet, Lieutenant General C. Hodges. The 8th Division was in the 7th Corps. So General Weaver had to go to the 7th Corps Headquarters and report to Major General "Lightning" Joe Collins, Commanding Officer, and I got to meet him, too.

Why did it seem important to me to meet generals? I had started as a private in the National Guard when I was only seventeen. I was commissioned five years later on active duty in the Army of the United States. From where I stood, generals were like movie stars. They had been to the best military schools, made soldiering their life work, and many of WWII's generals had lived through WWI, which was no easy job.

We arrived at 8th Division Headquarters, and the General made his presence known. A staff meeting was called to brief him on what our situation was and what the enemy was doing. We soon found out that the Hurtgen Forest was a terrible place to fight a battle. It was an area where a reforestation project had been going on for years. Some of the woods were so thick a man could hardly push his way through. It had been fought over, back and forth; mines had been laid all over the place and nobody knew where they were. The incoming artillery would burst in the trees, which was much more effective than bursting on the ground, sending tree limbs crashing down. The patrols that were sent out sometimes couldn't find their way back because of the thick undergrowth.

Our Headquarters was at a place called Rotgen. We operated from there for a while. There was so much to do to catch up with the new people, new areas, new regiments, new towns. One of the things the General insisted on was that I learn the names and pronunciation of all of the towns in our area so that he would know. Lammerdorf, Witzerath, Simmerat, Schmidt, Kommerscheidt, Untermoubach, Obermoubach, Bergstein, Brandenberg, Hurtgen, Vossenack, Germeter, Zweifall, Kornelimunster are examples of how well the Germans could confuse the ABCs.

In the new Golden Arrow 8th Infantry Division, I spent most of my free time with the G-2 learning where the safe roads were. The General daily wanted to go down into the regimental areas and battalion areas where there was action going on, but he didn't want me taking him on a road where he would get shot at—unless he knew we would get shot at no matter what to get where we were going. The G-2 was supposed to know these things. I spent time with the G-3 section to find out where the regimental and battalion headquarters *were.*

It was beginning to get much colder. Rain turned the walking paths into slop. The roads off of the black top had to be covered with logs to keep the trucks and tanks from getting stuck. The rain did not last for long after we arrived at the 8th Division. Around December 10 came the first freeze, and from then on each night instead of rain it snowed. It was so cold—sometimes you would just shake. The muscles across your chest would vibrate. I don't know how the people in the foxholes were able to stand the privation.

It was better in some respects after the freeze started because it was a cure for one of the enemies of the infantry soldier, trenchfoot. When for days you can't get your feet dry and you pull your foot out of a wet, soggy shoe and sock, your feet are white and wrinkled, and you have a very serious problem. I was lucky. I managed to get tank suits and rubber overshoes and one of those nice olive drab scarves for around the neck. The scarves proved their worth later on when it snowed every day. The snow would blow in around one's neck and the scarf would catch it.

I was introduced to another important task of my job. The word got around that Marlene Dietrich and Mitzi Mayberry, another actress, were close by. The General said, "Mayhall, go get them and bring them to the mess for lunch." Break out the champagne! The General told me to take his staff car. Perko and I went looking for two actresses. They were not hard to find, entertaining troops in a small town about ten miles away.

We picked them up and it turned out at the time that Marlene Dietrich was collecting unit shoulder patches. Nothing would do except she must collect my Golden Arrow 8th Infantry Division patch with the eight in the middle on a blue field

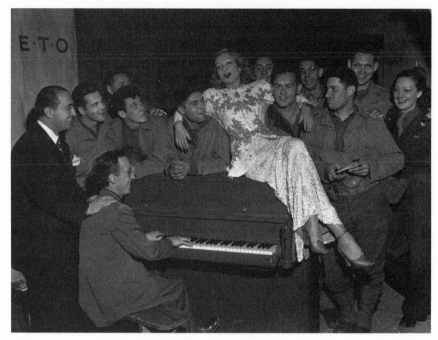

Above: Marlene Dietrich and Mitzi Mayberry (far right) entertain the troops; France, 1944. (Corbis)

shaped like a shield. I had to present her my knife. She said, "That's a little big," but she went to work cutting the threads to take my patch. While Marlene Dietrich was doing this, Mitzi Mayberry was hanging out the back door window whistling at the GIs. My social status had gone up considerably with Marlene Dietrich wanting and cutting off my shoulder patch.

I delivered the two ladies to Division Headquarters, and the General invited his staff officers to the mess for champagne and lunch. I was doing part of the pouring, and at first I was asking if they would care for more. The General took me to one side and said, "Don't ask, just pour if they are holding a glass."

After lunch, the driver and I took the ladies back to where transportation was waiting to take them where they would entertain more troops. Seeing them come to the front lines like that certainly gave me a new respect for Hollywood people.

Rumors were turning up with real disturbing regularity. The 8th Division had been in the line in the Bulge area before they moved north into the Hurtgen Forest. The G-2 had told me more than one time that the Germans were preparing something across the lines. The Germans were being very quiet about it. The G-2 (8th Division) had reported the activity up through channels, but no one in higher headquarters would believe that anything was going on. No one took the information seriously; we all just went about our business. Higher headquarters was using the Bulge area as a rest area. When a Division had been beaten up badly, they were sent into this nice, quiet part of the line where they could re-equip, retrain, and replace their missing people.

■　■　■

Silver Star

The General told me that he had received another medal, a French Croix-de-Guerre, and wanted me to go pick it up at 20th Corps Headquarters. The 20th Corps Headquarters was at Conflans at that time and was commanded by General Walker as one of General Patton's corps. Our 8th Division Headquarters was in Germany at a little town called Rott. I got a jeep and a driver from the motor pool, and we took off going south right across the front of where the German Bulge would be. We didn't think enough of the German big push to worry.

We got to the 20th Corps Headquarters and discovered the medal had been forwarded to the British 12th Army Group, commanded by General Montgomery. We came back through Bostoger across the Bulge area and then deep into Belgium to 12th Army Group. We found the right people, picked up the medal, and headed back to our division. It wasn't until after the German attack that I realized that the only thing that kept the jeep driver and me out of the Bulge fighting was lucky timing. We first crossed on the 27th of November and then crossed twice during the second week of December, only a few days before the German attack was executed.

I returned back to Division Headquarters and found that we were fighting aggressively all along our line. Just before the General took command, we had lost a battalion in an attack to capture Schmidt. Schmidt was the last big stronghold that stood in the way of capturing the great earthen dam at the head of the Roer River. The dam had enough water storage to flood the whole 1st Army front and the whole British 12th Army Group to our left in Belgium and Holland.

The 8th Division had made a penetration across the valley that separated Vossenack and Schmidt. They crammed tanks and men through the gap. It appeared that the division had done a great thing, but the road up out of the valley to the high ground of Schmidt gave way under the heavy tanks and rain. The Germans counterattacked, and we were not able to get enough of our heavy stuff up on the ridge in time to help. The Germans captured and killed a whole battalion of the 8th Division. We didn't know it at the time, but the road through Schmidt was one of the German supply lines for the Bulge. They could not let us capture it no matter the cost.

The General was briefed by the division staff, and then he went from regiment to regiment and from battalion to battalion to talk to each commander to find out what they thought about the situation and what we should do to improve it. Each time the General went, that meant I went, as well as Perko and Garman as a guard. Sometimes we had an extra jeep of guards. The jeep had a machine gun mounted on it, and a lot of the guards were experts with Tommy guns.

The Hurtgen Forest was a reforestation project that was about twenty or twenty-five years old. Acres of young pine and fur trees stood straight and tall and covered the ground with low and fallen branches. Visibility was bad. You couldn't see anything until you were on top of it. The Germans had stocked the forest with deer, elk, and wild boar. Moving, finding one's way, fighting in this thick cover was very difficult. There were few roads through the Hurtgen Forest, and they didn't seem to run the right way for our advance. Roads had to be cleared and small trees had to be cut and laid side-by-side to get trucks and guns into positions.

The first time I made a trip to the front with the General it was drizzling rain, as it seemed to do most of the time. The paths were ankle deep in mud. When you took your boots and socks off, your feet looked as if you had stayed in the bathtub too long. The foxholes were miserable, muddy, wet, and getting colder. It was not safe to stay out of the foxholes for long; the Germans were

Above: Chow is served to the men of the 347th Infantrymen Regiment on their way to La Roche, Belgium. January 13, 1945. (National Archives, NWDNS-111-SC-198849)

making sure that we stayed put. Artillery and mortar fire fell continually in some of the areas that we had captured.

The next time the General went down to the front, it had begun to snow. I guess it was a blessing in disguise, because everything froze up again: no more wet mud—just frozen mud. On this occasion, I came near being back in a company. The General was talking to a Battalion Commander and the Battalion Commanding Officer was telling the General that he needed replacements, both men and officers. He had received so much mortar and artillery fire during the night that he had lost six men wounded who had been in covered-over foxholes. The General asked him if he needed a good Company Commander.

As I was the only Company Commander he had around at the time, I reached for my carbine and was looking for anything else I wanted to keep with me. The Battalion Commanding Officer thought about it and shook his head. He had all the company commanders he needed. He wanted someone for them to command. The General replied that he would see if he couldn't shake up the replacement system some.

The division was trying to clean our sector of Germans on the west side of the Roer River. We were receiving so much artillery fire because we were on the north flank of the Bulge area. The Germans did not want us to cross the Roer River and get in behind their big operation. The little towns that the 8th Division had to take were Vossenack, Germeter, Hurtgen, Kleinhau, Brandenberg, and Bergstein; all these towns were on high ridges. We came out of the thick part of the forest at Germeter and took it first. Vossenack was taken one house at a time. It was a long town built on one street right down the top of a ridge. Not only were the Germans shooting at our advancing troops from the next house down, but they had observation on us from across two valleys and shot at the units from two directions.

Vossenack was a mean battle. Each time it looked like we were about to finish it, something else would pop up. When we had pushed, shot, run the Germans out of Vossenack, the Battalion Headquarters moved into a cellar facing Schmidt across a wide valley. The Germans opened fire with the famous deadly 88mms and put a shell right through the door and killed the whole battalion staff. A few days later the Germans started shipping soldiers behind our lines until they had enough to attack our position in Vossenack. We had lost so many men and we were so weak in manpower that a small task force had to be made up of cooks, typists, MPs, and mechanics.

This little task force was led by a motor pool officer, but it successfully hit the Germans on their flank and killed or captured the entire enemy force. The motor pool officer was a true leader; with his Tommy Guns, he ran from place to place, foxhole to foxhole. It was such an outstanding act of heroism and leadership that he was decorated with a Distinguished Service Cross, the second-highest award for bravery in action.

Vossenack had been taken, but it still was not a place where one could walk around in the daytime. The Germans had observation on it from Schmidt and Bergstein, their snipers were very good, and that 88mm gun that they had made our soldiers dig their foxholes "Hail Mary" deep.

Then—the question of how we were going to take Hurtgen. Our only approach in that direction had been blocked by a tank-killing, road-cratering, smart trick. On this road going from Germeter to Hurtgen, the Germans had dug in six Tellermines and run a stick like a broom handle straight down. One end of the stick was on the activator of the mine and the other end pointed up into the road, but couldn't be seen or detected by a mine detector. A tank ran over this mine-trap, the tank was blown all apart, and the men in it were also. I saw the head and arm of one man in a tree at least fifty yards from the road. There was a hole in the road big enough to drop four or five cars in. The engineers were put

Below: Allied soldiers do laundry in a captured German pillbox. (FDR Library)

Above: Engineers of the 75th Division, Co. C, 275th Engineers, sweep a snow-covered road for enemy mines. (US Military History Institute)

to work repairing this road and making it ready for our advance on Hurtgen.

As the plan worked out, it was necessary to take all four of the towns at one time. It turned out that the ridges around Hurtgen were clear of woods because it was a farming area, and Brandenberg was the same. The elevation of Hurtgen, Kleinhau, Brandenberg, and Bergstein was about the same, and if the attack were made on Hurtgen alone, it could be shot at from Kleinhau, Brandenberg, Bergstein, and from across the valley from Schmidt. A plan was developed for the Combat Command Regiment (CCR), a tank unit that was attached to the 8th Division, and part of our infantry units to go barreling up the Germeter-Hurtgen-Kleinhau road shooting everything, running over everything. Then they were to turn right at the crossroads and take Brandenberg and Bergstein all in one day-long movement.

CCR didn't like the plan, because there were too many enemy antitank weapons. The houses in Hurtgen all had root cellars that the Germans used for pillboxes and which made very strong defensive positions. All around Hurtgen there were open fields, so the German defensive fire would be terrible on our troops.

The day came for the attack, and the engineers went out with their mine detectors and swept the road as far as they could for the tankers. It was still dark early morning, and the CCR commander wanted it swept again, and the story goes that an engineer tied a frying pan onto a stick and went out and swept the road with a frying pan.

The attack took off. The tanks went in firing at anything that moved; an 8th Division infantry company that had been strengthened to 200 men came out of the woods to make the infantry assault on Hurtgen, and the town was taken even under fire from the Germans. It was a real slug-fest; some of our tanks were knocked out in the middle of Hurtgen and in the fields around it. There were very few of the 8th Division infantry company who were not killed or wounded in the attack.

The General wanted to see how the attack was going, so we left Headquarters around noon and went into Hurtgen. There was still rifle fire, machine-gun fire, and some artillery fire coming in from the Schmidt area. At the first house we stopped and went to the cellar.

Of all places to run into a former brother officer from the old 156th Infantry. His name was Alfred G. Francis. I had known him since the old National Guard days. We didn't have much time to talk; the General called me and told me he wanted to find the Battalion Commander. The General needed to get there in a hurry because our offensive needed more troops, more fire-power to complete the capture of Brandenberg and Bergstein. I told the General I would go forward and find out where that officer had his Command Post.

I climbed out of the cellar and so did the General, and he watched me go. As I got close to a tank that was still burning, the Germans fired a couple of rounds close by; I ducked behind the tank, which infantry people don't do very often because tanks draw fire. I waited a few minutes and then went on. I wondered who was doing all the shooting, because I couldn't see anybody. Finally, I came to the Catholic church. The roof was shot off, all the windows broken. It must have been a nice little church at one time. I ran into a soldier there, and asked him where the Battalion C.P. was. His directions led me next door, and I went back into the street and directed the General into the root cellar where the C.P. was.

Apparently, I was not aware of the amount of fire that was going on around me at the time I left the General and went off across the open space looking for the Battalion C.P. The General was impressed, and later on I was decorated. A Silver Star!

■ ■ ■

The battle roared on for the rest of the day, and we took Brandenberg and Bergstein, but by the time we had taken Bergstein we were so weakened we were having trouble holding it. The Germans were counterattacking. We got some help from the big fighter planes, Thunderbolts, during this time. The fighter planes were diving in, their eight 50-caliber machine guns firing into the Germans, helping to slow the counterattack.

The next day I was passing through the radio room in Division Headquarters, and I stopped to listen to a conversation between a Ground-Air Liaison and a Flight Leader. The Liaison Officer was in a Sherman tank, and he was in considerable trouble, and he was calling for help from the flight of P-47s that was supposed to be supporting us this day.

The ground-to-air forward observer called to the P-47 flight leader, "Blue Flight Leader, come help me. I'm in this Sherman tank on the east side of this two story building."

The Blue Flight Leader answered him, "What's the matter, little friend?"

"Blue Flight Leader, there's a German Tiger tank on the other side of this building that is about to get me."

The Blue Flight Leader said, "Little friend, if I bomb that Tiger tank, I'll probably get you, too."

The Forward Observer replied, "If you don't get the Tiger tank, *he'll* get me." Blue Flight Leader came in, and bombed and knocked out the Tiger.

The battle went on. Our troops had become so few, the General asked Corps if the battalion of Rangers that were camped in our area could be used to help us out. Permission was granted. That night, the Ranger battalion attacked. They were running when they crossed the Line of Departure. They swept the Bergstein Hill and killed or captured all of the Germans who were still trying to get Bergstein. I was told some of them went down to the Roer River and got a bucket of water just to prove they had run the Germans out.

It came home to me that the Ranger battalions were a special type of unit, special training, special people.

A week later I met a young fighter pilot captain, Quentin C. Aanenson, who had finished his fifty missions and had come up to be an air-ground coordinator while waiting for transportation home. I told him about the business of Blue Flight Leader bombing the tank in our fight for Bergstein, and he said, "Van, that was me."

We held all of our ground from then on. On December 16 the Germans made their big attack; it was terrible for the divisions in front of their offensive. The 99th Division got chewed up something awful. The 106th Division lost identification of two regiments, and the Third regiment was shot up badly. The 28th Division and the 4th Division that had been put into that quiet area to rest and refit were both torn up, disorganized, pushed back.

The 8th Division was to the northern side of the German Bulge. We had German paratroopers running around behind us, but we were only delayed by the Bulge. We had to stop and wait until the German advance attack was contained. General Weaver gave orders that we would not give them "one damn foot"—that we would dig one reserve line after another in case we had to fall back. Then he passed down that any man who got two confirmed kills got to go to Paris for a week.

Two confirmed kills meant someone had to be watching and would be willing to swear to the fact. So we developed a lot of snipers.

We were continually going to the front talking to the regimental and battalion commanders trying to keep the fighting spirit of the unit up. Waiting in snow country makes everybody careless. We were doing everything we could to maintain morale. The division found a place where we could pull men out of the lines back to where they could get a hot bath, fresh clothes, dry socks, and hot meals. Everybody couldn't go at once; a few were pulled out of companies and platoons at a time.

The General, Perko, Garman, and I were up front. The General wanted to check on how these new defensive lines and foxholes were being done. We arrived shortly after a man had stepped on an antipersonnel mine along the Germeter Ridge. The area had been fought over so much that mines were planted everywhere. In the back-and-forth of the fighting, we lost track of where we had put mines down and didn't know at all where the Germans had put them. This soldier was just doing his job; he was digging a foxhole, got too hot, and walked over to a fence post to hang his coat. That was the mistake: the mine he stepped on was in between where he was digging and where the post was. From a distance he looked like just another KIA. A sergeant who was there said he had checked him, and he was dead. I always wondered if that sergeant had really crossed the mined area and checked him. I have felt bad many times thinking I had the opportunity to check to see if he was dead, and I didn't.

The Battle of the Bulge raged on to the south of us. Our division and corps were hunting for the English-speaking, American-uniformed German paratroopers who were running around cutting communication lines, changing road signs, and killing a few of our people as they went. 1st Army moved in what troops we could to keep the Germans from turning north into the large supply areas around Liège, Belgium.

The weather was in the Germans' favor from the day they attacked until the day before Christmas. It snowed, great sheets like fog that covered the whole area of attack. Our airfields were socked in. Even when the planes could get off the ground, they couldn't find the battle.

The German planes flew along our front, strafing us. The planes were getting real personal. In a forward area a group of ME 109s came sweeping up a valley, shooting as they came. I didn't have anything but my .45 pistol, and I was shooting that. All around me men jumped on their trucks, mounted 50-caliber machine guns, and blasted away. If any were hit, they didn't slow down. The flyers made another pass a little later on their way back into Germany, but we were better prepared. Everybody popped off at them with something.

A few days later, I was on the road between Zweifall and Aachen when two Folke-Wolf 190s decided to strafe the road. We heard them coming and stopped the jeep on the inside of a curve behind a building and let them go by. Those 20mms they were firing threw little pieces of shrapnel all over the place. After the FW 190s strafed the road, and we had gone on to where we were going and to the same curve in the road on the way back, here they came again. The driver and I dove out of the jeep and lay flat behind a stone wall. Bullets from the two planes slapped into the two-story building across the street. It was both exciting and scary to be lying there with the planes' guns pounding away. After they had gone, I felt the need to thumb my nose at them—and take off quick before they came back.

The Battle of the Bulge was slowing to an end, and we were slowing also. More orders came down and new plans were being made. The 8th Division was to spread out to the north along the Roer River, taking Oberman Untermanbach. We had already moved our Division HQ. We had procured, taken away, otherwise run the Mayor of Zweifall out of his house. It was a nice two-story house with hot and cold water—the only house I was in that had running hot water and a bath tub. But the General wanted to be farther forward, so the HQ moved down into the woods. The General had a trailer he liked, and the engineers were ordered to build enough log cabins for the division staff. I had a small cabin between the General's trailer and the log cabin that was built for the staff mess hall.

In the mess hall in the Hurtgen Forest I learned to like piano music. I had gotten a piano from somewhere, and we had two men who were great on it. One could play anything you could whistle, and the other played nothing but classical music. Each night one or the other would be playing in the mess hall when the General and the staff came in to eat. This was our only entertainment since Marlene Dietrich and Mitzi Mayberry came to visit.

Right before the HQ was moved down into the woods, I had met my old Baton Rouge friend Killer Woods. Killer was a great ping-pong player back in our YMCA days, and that's where his nickname came from—his overhand smash. Killer Woods came up one night as a replacement Platoon Leader. I had seen him long enough to say "Hello."

December 24: The sun came up. The fog rolled out and from our division you could see the vapor trails of our planes over the Bulge for the first time. It raised everybody's spirits. I had an extra bottle of something, so I decided to bring it down to Lieutenant Woods for a Christmas present and to help get some of the frost and snow out of his system. The General's secretary asked me to take him with me; he had never seen up front and wanted to go so bad. He was afraid that he would only be able to tell his family and children that he fought the war with his typewriter. We got permission for him to go with us. Off we went to find Killer Woods.

We got to Brandenberg and found out that he was with a platoon at Bergstein. We were getting ready to leave for Bergstein when the Regimental Commander appeared and asked what was the visit was for. I told the Colonel about my friend, and he said, "Wait. The Germans are still shooting at people down in Bergstein in the daytime." The Colonel had someone phone down to the battalion and to the company and found that Killer Woods had been wounded and had gone back to the hospital. I thanked the Colonel, gave him the bottle of Scotch, and wished him a Merry Christmas.

We started out of Brandenberg on the first day the sky had cleared since the 16th of December. It was such a beautiful day that one was glad to be alive anywhere. Then I heard some machine-gun and rifle fire to the north by the Roer River, and I thought it would be nice to go up on Hill 401 and see what we could see. The secretary was having fun; he had seen Vossenack, Germeter, Hurtgen where he knew much fighting had gone on. He had seen burned-out tanks, trucks—there was even a shot-down German ME 109 out in a field. We didn't go near the 109 in the daytime; it was under observation by the Germans and they enjoyed shooting at any dummy who walked out into the open.

Hill 401 looked nice and peaceful. Jeeps and people were going back and forth on the German side of it, and everything seemed quiet enough and safe enough. So we went up, and there were some artillery people with a Battery Commander's tele-scope looking to the east.

Below: GIs are silhouetted against a sky streaked with vapor trails from Allied and enemy planes on the first clear day during the Battle of the Bulge. (National Archives, NWDNS-111-SC-197661)

They said they hadn't seen anything, so I asked if I could look through the scope. I sat down behind the B.C. Scope (which I had been introduced to in the artillery at LSU) and I looked toward Schmidt, across the Roer River and out on the Cologne plain. I was enjoying this until I took a second look across the Roer River, at the hills just as high as the one I was sitting on. I got the queasy feeling in my stomach that I was looking into a German scope across the river. I hadn't any more than thought that thought when I heard a field gun go off, and I heard the shell coming. That shell burst very close. It was too big for a 105mm.

It was time to move. I turned, and the secretary was right behind me, and we ran behind an old shot-up radio shack. We stayed there for a while, and then I started down off the hill. As soon as I came out from behind the radio shack, I heard the gun go off again, and here came the shell, and I dove into a shell hole. I stayed in the shell hole. I counted to ten. Nothing happened. I came out of the shell hole, and that gun fired again, and that shell was coming, and I dove for another shell hole. I stayed in that shell hole for a count of twenty, and as I came out that gun went off again, and that shell was on its way again, and I was diving for cover again. Somewhere there was a German observer who was having a lot of fun, laughing like hell.

From where I was, I could see no humor in the situation. For about 300 yards I was in and out of shell holes. Shells were landing between thirty and sixty yards from me each time they exploded. I finally got to the edge of the little town of Kleinhau and dove into a cellar. I found my jeep driver there, and then got to looking for the secretary and the one guard who had come with us. I looked back the way I had come and saw two heads poking up out of holes. I waved at them to come on, and they did. The guard was glad to leave where he was; he had jumped into a machine-gun pit from which a dead German had not been removed. It seemed to quiet down after that, and we got into the jeep and went on back to Division HQ. The secretary did not ask me for any more visits to the front.

Above: Silver Star presentation. Left to right: General Weaver, Van Mayhall, John Garman, John Perko, and unidentified man.

It had never occurred to me that anything was going to happen to me. I had seen so many dead Germans, dead and wounded Americans—but the thought of something happening to me was very farfetched. However, after that artillery experience on Hill 401 in the Hurtgen Forest, from then on, when I came out of a hole, cellar, or a door, my stomach tightened, and I was listening for that gun to go off.

■ ■ ■

The General's Packard

*A*s everywhere else, it is timing that gets people killed or lets them escape. Down in the valley between Vossenack and Schmidt there was an inn. I do not believe either the Americans or the Germans stayed in the inn because it was right on our front lines. It was not a place that could be defended. The importance of the inn was that it had a coal pile. It was so cold that the Germans and the Americans would dig holes for protection from the weather and cover the top of them over with logs. When the holes got big, a fire would be needed to keep warm, to cook, to warm coffee, and to dry socks. Then the word would be passed—"Let's go get some coal at the inn," and off they would go on completely unauthorized patrol. They would do their very best to be quiet. However, about that same time of night some Germans would get cold, too, and come down to get coal. When the Germans and the Americans met at the coal pile, there would be one hell of a shoot-out. On the occasions of the coal-pile battles at least they knew what they were killing each other for.

The 8th Division went to work, cleared the Germans out of Germeter, Vossenack, Hurtgen, Kleinhau, Brandenberg, Bergstein, and cleared the Germans in our sector back across the Roer River.

Christmas came. General Weaver made sure that every man up front got hot turkey and all the trimmings for Christmas dinner. Somebody suggested that there should be a party at Division Headquarters. The General liked the party idea, and we all went to work preparing. We were in the best quarters that we had ever had. We had the Mayor's house, with electricity, hot water, and heat. The kitchen crew outdid themselves in preparing party food for the staff and the nurses who were coming from a hospital back behind the lines. How the nurses got there, I do not know, but they had broken out their best uniforms and perfume. It was a shock to smell perfume after months of smelling death and gun smoke.

The party went well, and the time came for the nurses to go back to the hospital, and the person who had brought them seemed to have disappeared. So the General said, "Mayhall, take the nurses back. Use the Packard."

This floored me, for I hadn't seen the Packard. When did it get here? Who brought it? Of course, I was delighted. The only car that had parked in front of the Mayhall house was my brother's Model T. Dad was a railroad man, and it didn't occur to him that he needed a car. Mother didn't see the need for a car; she didn't want to drive one of those things. The grocery store

Below: Christmas in a cabin in the Hurtgen Forest, 1944. Wrapping paper from food packages was used to line the walls for warmth.

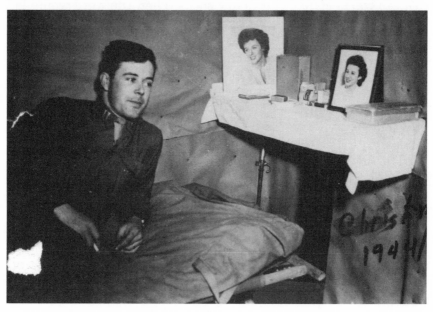

was only three blocks, and all the other stores were on Third Street, only six blocks away. There was another little thing called the Depression; everyone was having a problem with shortage of money for luxuries.

By Christmas 1944, I had been driving jeeps, all sizes of trucks—I had even gotten around to driving a tank with a self-propelled 105mm. I had driven the staff car to escort Marlene Dietrich and Mitzi Mayberry. I had no doubt that I could drive the Packard to the hospital and back. I was still surprised the car was there and wondered how the Packard had followed us to Zweifall.

So, off we went—the nurses and I headed to the Packard, and there were "ohs and ahs" from the nurses, for they had been riding around in jeeps and trucks since they left the States. We turned onto the snow-covered road leading back to the hospital, and everything seemed to be going fine until we were about four or five miles from the Headquarters. All of a sudden a great cloud of smoke filled the inside of the car. I jumped out and opened the trunk. Some loose wires must have crossed and sparked; a fire was raging in there. Gasoline and rags were in flames, and I expected the gas tank to explode any minute.

"Get out!" I yelled to the nurses. "It's going to explode!" I got the nurses out of the Packard and at least fifty yards away. I didn't realize that I had left my nice warm, fur-lined coat in the car until I began to shiver and shake from the cold. Ammunition began to explode inside the car, and I knew I had left my pistol on the front seat as well.

Well, we sat there and watched that damned Packard burn down to its rims. It never exploded like they always do in the picture shows. I was disgusted that I had told the nurses it was going to explode.

We were lucky. The military police back at Headquarters saw the light from the fire and came to investigate. I asked them to take the nurses on to the hospital, and I went back to the 8th Division Headquarters. Everyone in the place was asleep by that time, so I didn't try to make a report. I sort of wished that I had gone with the nurses to the hospital. I knew all hell was going to open up the next morning.

I made a bad mistake at breakfast. When General Weaver came in we all stood up as normal, and when the General sat down, I said, "General, catch on to the table."

He caught hold of the table and he said, "Now what?"

I gave him the news about his Packard. I should have waited until he had had some coffee or something. The General sort of looked like a skyrocket fixing to go off, and then he lit into me about "driving down the main street in Berlin," and a number of other things. He finally closed with the order, "You are going to walk from now on when I go to inspect the regiments and battalions."

So, at 0800 hours that morning the jeep was loaded and General Weaver came walking out, and I was standing at attention and saluting, and he repeated, "You walk." The jeep took off, and I took off walking right after them. I had walked about three miles when I realized I was dressed for riding in an open jeep and not for walking. I stripped off the tank suit and a little bit of the sweat began to dry off.

The second headquarters the General was going to was about twelve miles from the first. When I got there the General had been and left. The Colonel there said, "Mayhall, you'd better let me find out where General Weaver is; it's getting dark, and people shoot at people walking around in the dark out there." The Colonel phoned around and found out the General was heading back to Division Headquarters. The Colonel said, "I'll send you back to Division in my jeep."

I said, "Colonel, I do appreciate it, but he said 'Walk!'"

I didn't think it was a good idea to go back the way I came, so I took what I knew to be a shortcut. This forest had deer, elk, wild boar, and some Germans moving around in the snow. With a little wind, snow falling off of limbs, one's own imagination, one wonders what each noise out in the dark can be. I kept walking, and it got darker and darker—and there was more movement and noise from different sides of the road. I managed not to run. Fortunately I came out of the shortcut right at one of the MP posts that protected our main route for supply. I was happy they hadn't opened fire on this loner walking out of the dark, and they seemed to be glad to have some strange company. It was about 2000 hours, and I had arrived about the time their hot food came up, and I was very glad to be invited to eat with them.

At about this time, people at Division Headquarters began to wonder where I was. The information that I was missing was telephoned around to the forward MP posts. The MP Sergeant who answered the phone where I was eating looked around and said, "You must be Captain Mayhall. Someone at Division is looking for you." The Sergeant reported I was there and he would send me back with the next Motor Patrol.

I reported to the Chief of Staff and went to bed. The next morning I was standing at attention and saluting when General Weaver came down. I was fully ready to walk again, but he looked at me and said, "Mayhall, get in the damned jeep."

■ ■ ■

Crossing

After Christmas, we began to get more replacements. General Weaver recognized that we were losing too many new replacements because of the terrible change of coming from peaceful areas behind the lines into the front lines where each man had to cope with freezing foxholes and the complete boredom of inactivity contrasted with the startling and fearsome shell-fire explosions, mortar fire, machine-gun fire, rifle fire, sounds of heavy vehicles. It is a matter of good training and indoctrination to keep a soldier as an effective fighting member of a team. General Weaver was the only Division Commander I met that ran this kind of school as new replacements came up.

As the Battle of the Bulge wore on, General Eisenhower called in the army commanders to decide what to do and when it should be done. The Germans were getting farther into the Allied lines; they wanted to split the Allied forces. If they reached Brussels and then Antwerp, they would have the whole 1st Army cut off. Brussels and Antwerp were centers of supply. The 1st Army was blocking on the north to keep the Germans from Liège, a large supply center. The British were digging in along the Meuse River to block further movement to the west. When General Eisenhower told General Patton that he would have to thin his lines and pull divisions out to attack the southern shoulder of the Bulge and relieve Bastogne, General Patton told General Eisenhower that the movement had already been started, and part of his army was already on the road.

It was a terrible move. It was cold. It snowed most of the time. Everything was iced over. Trucks slipped off the road, tanks broke down, men's feet were cold and sore. Lots of the men had fever—didn't even know they were sick; they just thought they were cold. If contact could have been made with the Germans and fighting could have carried on until somebody had won, it may or may not have been so bad. Oh, the days and hours that I spent trying to keep face, ears, and hands warm and still hold back the chills that would run through my chest muscles! Now I knew what Valley Forge was like.

Patton pulling part of his army out of the line and turning them north to attack the southern shoulder and relieve Bastogne doesn't sound like too much of a trick. However, there are a few details involved in making a move like that. There are thousands of soldiers to consider; these soldiers had to cover many miles. The infantry is happy to ride, but they are designed to walk. They must be served food; they must be supplied with clothes that can protect them in the winter weather. These are night-and-day clothes, for there are no pajamas out in the snow. There are hundreds of vehicles that have to keep rolling, needing gas, oil, grease and tires. Hundreds of tanks have to be gassed, oiled, maintained, supplied with ammunition. In a corps or army, there are a lot of people whose job is to do nothing but keep the movement going in the right direction. Whatever difficulties the 3rd Army had in getting there, they came in walking and rolling and, most important, they came in shooting.

Anyway, a good part of the 3rd Army arrived. They attacked the southern shoulder of the Bulge, and they did relieve Bastogne, the 3rd Army attacking from the south, the 1st Army blocking and attacking on the north side. When the weather cleared on Christmas Eve, Allied air forces came down on the German forces like "ducks on June bugs." The Germans dropped nearly everything they had brought with them and headed for Germany. A lot of them didn't make it. The Americans followed them.

General Weaver had a minor heart attack that didn't slow him down a bit. A month later the 8th Division got new warning orders. "Be prepared to shift to the north. Clean out all Germans west of the Roer River and be prepared to force a crossing." General Weaver started pulling one regiment out of the line at a time to let them refit and retrain and get some replacements.

The river that we were planning to cross had snow on the banks down to the water line, so we did not practice in the water. The practice came in learning to carry assault boats down a marked trail to the water in the dark of night. All supporting mortars, machine guns, and field guns had to be in place to start shooting to the far bank and walking that fire ahead of the landing parties to give them protection as they came out of the boats and up the banks.

We only had one bridge site in our area and that was at a town called Duren. The Germans had blown the center span out of the bridge. All we had to do was to put a Bailey bridge together and push it across the bridge where the span was blown out.

The third night was coming with our bridge still not in place. The General was mad as a wet hen and said to me, "Let's go get that damn bridge in." It was near midnight when we left Division Headquarters and went to the bridge site. Nothing was going on. No work going on. No shells coming in. The General said, "Mayhall, find those engineers right now."

I found the engineers right quick and sent the Lieutenant commanding the engineers to the General. The General asked for an explanation and the Lieutenant told him the Germans had been shelling them all day. The General said, "There's no shells coming in now; and what's more, I am going to stand on that damned bridge until you push it across."

Well, I didn't think the General should be standing on that bridge by himself, so the two of us went out together. We didn't know how many Germans were left across the river where we were trying to get, but I began to think about it every time the General pulled out his Zippo lighter to light a cigarette. Over that dark river it looked like a 100-watt bulb. Each time he lit a cigarette, I thought, "They will shoot him off this time." It never occurred to me that I might get hit too, but as I looked down into the cold Roer River, I thought I would have a terrible time getting him out of that water.

The bridge was pushed across the river and the bridge boarded all the way across. The reserve regiment that was waiting on the ridge was committed at daylight. This reserve regiment spread out in front of Duren and shot their way through. By that night all of Duren belonged to us.

The General left the bridge before I did, and when I came off, the Corps Commander, General "Lightning Joe" Collins, was having a conversation with him. General Weaver had been in combat all the way across France from late June, 1944, to now, February 22, 1945. Which meant that, for a man his age, he was beginning to wear a little thin. He had a little heart trouble, but he wouldn't let that stop him. What went on between General Collins and General Weaver I do not know, but when we got back to Division, I had a copy of my new orders:

> *You will escort General Weaver to Brooke General Hospital at Fort Sam Houston, Texas. You will return to your Division within ten days after the General is in Fort Sam Houston.*

It didn't take long to put one's stuff together and leave in the Army. We departed the front lines on the 26th of February and we stopped at the field hospital in Liège, Belgium, for the General to be examined. From there we went to the Military Hospital in Paris, France, for the General to be further examined. It was too long a trip for the General to go all the way to Paris from Liège in one day, so we stopped off in Reims, France, the champagne capital of Europe. The General had been there during WWI and didn't want to go home without going by to see what he could see. He picked up a case of pink champagne, and the next day we went on to Paris. The General wanted to get checked over in Paris and say good-bye to his old friends and see Paris one more time. He didn't plan on coming back.

We got the General settled in the hospital and I started looking for some of my old outfits from Louisiana. I finally found

Above: Bailey bridge under construction for the Third Army. (Corbis/Hulton-Deutsch Collection)

Major Cassaigne from New Orleans, who had been a Company Commander in the 156th Infantry like I was.

George H. Cassaigne wasn't afraid of anything. He had also been the only officer in the 156th Infantry Regiment who seemed to enjoy classical music. He had a player and records and we often heard his music at odd hours of the day and night. He soon developed into the Commanding Officer's troubleshooter. When a unit seemed to be slacking off, the Colonel would call George in to straighten it out. George was a big man, two-hundred-thirty pounds, with a tough countenance. He would walk in and announce that he was the new Company Commander, and all of a sudden things would start changing—better haircuts, closer shaves, standing at attention a little straighter, saluting a little sharper, beds made tighter, shoes and buttons shined brighter, details done faster, company streets cleaned cleaner, and even the kitchen turned out better food.

George was sent to England for security details around the big headquarters in London, for General Rogers' headquarters as I understood it. He did a fine job. His troops were clicking their heels, snapping fast salutes, giving a double sir. George was a Major by the time the headquarters moved to Paris, and he was still furnishing security.

When I looked up George, he was living in a great big beautiful place with all kinds of people running in and out. He was glad to see somebody from the old regiment.

Someone must have gotten to him about what he was going to tell his grandchildren. He had been living the life of Reilly from the time he arrived in London and he was still going strong in Paris, but he hadn't seen much in the way of war. As soon as I found him, he started pleading with me to get him out of Paris into a front-line division. He knew that an Aide-de-Camp to a Major General knows a lot of people. I told him

Below: General Weaver's farewell party. Capt. Mayhall only managed to get his eyes and nose into the photo.

people were getting shot, killed, to say nothing about getting the hell scared out of them. Nothing would do except I should try to get him into a combat outfit.

George said, "Van, I gotta get out of Paris. I gotta get up front."

I said, "You don't want to go where I've been. I told you: People are getting muddy, cold, wet, bruised, wounded, and killed. It's very easy to get those Purple Hearts."

"Be serious," he said. "I have to get out of Paris."

So I told him, " I have to go back to Division for business for the General. They're always looking for people who want to get into the front lines."

Well, the next day the General sent me back to the 8th Division Headquarters to pick up his paperwork. I got a driver and a jeep from a motor pool and took off. It was a long, cold trip. The division had all crossed the Roer River and taken off fast on the autobahn for Cologne, Germany, right on the Rhine River, and that is where I caught up with them. The Remagen bridge had been captured and American troops were pouring across. I had dinner with the division that night.

The new General was ready to put me right to work as an Assistant G-3. I told the General I thanked him much, but I still had to go to Fort Sam Houston first.

While I was in Cologne I went to Lt. Col. Edwin W. Grenelle, G-1 (Personnel). I turned in George's name, rank, and serial number and told the G-1 George needed something to tell his grandchildren. Lt. Col. Grenelle said he could use some good Majors. It worked out very well; before we left Paris, Major Cassaigne was transferred to the 8th Infantry, and he took our vehicles back to the division.

■ ■ ■

Paris in the Spring

I returned from my trip back to the 8th Infantry in Cologne, Germany. Everybody in our party was running from one amusement to the next and sleeping late. We were very lucky General Eisenhower's staff had an open ear for wherever and whatever General Weaver wanted to go and do. The General would say, "Mayhall, call Major Butcher [General Eisenhower's aide], tell him we would like tickets to the Follies Bergère." The Follies Bergère was probably the most popular show in Paris, and tickets were hard to come by, but not for Major Butcher! It is just *possible* that we have had shows on Broadway comparable to the Follies Bergère, but not *probable*. I visited Napoleon's Tomb, I walked by the Seine River, walked across the Place de la Concorde into Notre Dame. I had to see Notre Dame again. I saw the outside of the Louvre but time was getting short, and I didn't go in.

After two weeks in Paris the General was ready to go to London, and he wanted to stay there for a while. Most of the friends that I had known in England had packed up and gone to France, but I saw a few and saw my cousin Elizabeth Ann, the British pilot's wife. I gave the burp gun I had taken as a souvenir from Fort Koenigsmacher to a friend who had never been close to the front. I am sure he told his friends back home he had taken it away from a German. He was a Texan and they are prone to telling stories. I had an apartment on Moonstreet across from Hyde Park. All of the air defence guns in Hyde Park had been moved to the continent.

It was great to be in London at this time because of three things. One: The last of the German V-2 Rocket bombs came in.

Our armies on the continent had uncovered all of their launching sites and captured what was left of them. It was not too nice for the square block that the V-2 exploded in, but it was the last one that would fall on England. Two: For the nearly two years that I had visited London, there was terrible darkness—no house lights, no street lights, and no car lights. I was there when the lights came on again. It was so beautiful! Third: The church bells began to ring, the little bells, the medium bells, and the large bells of Big Ben and St. Paul's Cathedral. The world was on "Come back."

Our time in London was wearing out, and we were looking west. The General didn't want to fly home from England, so we were given passage on the *Ile de France*. *Ile de France* was one of the best and largest passenger ships that France had at that time. It was a fast ship that made the crossing without escort. We travelled to Glasgow, Scotland, where the ship was berthed.

I was so happy to get this passage to New York. We were due to arrive on April 25, 1945, the third anniversary of my wedding to Marie. I thought it would be wonderful to phone Marie and tell her I was home for our anniversary.

I was not quite over the War; the last month in the lines had done things that nobody understands unless they were there. I went to see a doctor the first day on board the *Ile de France,* because I had a bad cold and was hoping he could help. After I had talked with him for a while, he decided, "Mayhall, we've got to do something about you before you blow your top. You come in and see me every day on this trip, and we might get you calmed down." The doctor thought I was uptight and my nerves could be improved if he furnished me with a little medicinal alcohol each session. The doctors were supplied with some very good calming-down juice; I don't know what he said to me during those visits that helped, but I guess that big daily slug of medicinal alcohol was the ticket to climb down to near normal.

We landed in New York after we had waved to and cried over the Statue of Liberty. Lady Liberty seemed to be glad to see us back and, by the wet eyes of the people who were standing around me, there were a lot of soldiers who were glad to see her, too. The *Ile de France* was escorted into her berth, and it didn't take long for us to get off. A Red Cross lady handed me a pint of milk, the first whole milk I had seen or tasted in two and a half years! I drank it down with gusto.

I don't know how the Army takes care of so many details, but there was private transportation waiting for General Weaver and the rest of us that took us straight to Hollanden General Hospital. The General was already signed in and his room was waiting. We tucked him into his room, and as soon as he looked like he would stay there for a while, I went searching for a telephone. I found one at the end of the hall. I didn't know how to manage the dial, so I told the operator I had been overseas for two and a half years and I wanted to talk to my wife. She said, "Where is she?" I said, Baton Rouge, Louisiana, 537 Government Street.

It seemed like a train thundering down a track—"Priority Call, Priority Call." The connections switched and clicked and lines connected and finally a telephone answered. "Mrs. Van Mayhall? Captain Mayhall wants to talk to you."

I had been away from the South so long I never imagined what Marie would sound like. When I heard her voice, I couldn't believe this was Marie—no one could sound like a Hollywood picture show Southern girl like that. I was so shocked I hardly knew what to say. I said I had hoped to call on our anniversary, but head winds had made the *Ile de France* a day late. I told her I loved her and missed her, and for her to meet me in San Antonio at Brooke General Hospital.

The General's ailments were apparently not crippling. While I was doing business with the two pilots who had a Hudson, a two-motored airplane, waiting for us at the airport, the General decided to check out the clubs and restaurants that he hadn't seen since he was a much younger officer. The West Point boys of his time had enjoyed visiting New York for fun and games. In the infantry when a man gets to be fifty-six years old, he has to find a job or place in the organization where he can ride and sit, not walk, march, run, climb, dig, crawl, or swim. But, young at heart, the General knew that this might be his last time to see New York. After three days of enjoying New York, we got him on the plane.

General Weaver, Perko, Garman, two pilots, and myself took off from New York and headed south. After getting into the air the pilots were warned to land at Greenville, North Carolina, because of a bad weather front. Down we came, with rooms waiting for us to spend the night.

When the General and I said goodnight, he said, "Well, I guess the fun is over with."

I supposed he was referring to the war, because war is the only thing I have ever been involved in that took one hundred percent of your attention, time, abilities, and nerves.

The next morning we flew around the southern end of the Appalachians and then turned west across Alabama and Mississippi. We crossed Louisiana and the Mississippi River where the river poured through the Bonnet Spillway, and we flew on into Texas.

We landed somewhere at San Antonio, and everything was still laid on to get the General to Brooke General Hospital at Fort Sam Houston. With this done, I had other things to think about. I had told Marie to meet me at the hospital, so I went looking for her. I felt sure that she was there. I left the General with his wife in his room and went searching. I went into the hall and headed for the elevators to the lobby. The elevator doors opened for me, and there Marie stood in all of her young beauty. I didn't know how she would accept me because I was bigger than I had ever been, more serious, more intense and half crazy. We left the elevator and found a bench, and we sat and talked for a while. I didn't mention at the time that I had orders to be back in Europe in ten days.

After two and a half years of being apart, we were almost like strangers. We kissed and hugged, but this was 1945—great expressions of passion were not displayed in public.

We left our bench after a little while so I could introduce Marie to the General. I never knew what Marie thought of the General on that first meeting, but I did know what the old wolf thought of her.

As days wore on, Mrs. Weaver and General Weaver became more like second parents to us. Anything that they could do for us was done: rooms at the Officers Club, breakfast in bed. . . . On some nights we all came together for dinner in the Club.

About this time there was great celebration at wonderful news that had come over the War Department wires. Billy, General Weaver's son, had been one of a group of young officers sent on a

Above: 1200 POWs celebrate their freedom from a camp at Limburg, Germany. March 28, 1945. (National Archives, NLR-PHOCO-6654(40))

daring and dangerous mission before we left Europe. The mission was to break through the German lines to capture a POW camp full of Americans before the Germans could move them farther into Germany. The operation had at first been a success. The Americans punched a big hole in the German lines that they were never able to close up. The American task force captured the POW camp, but there was a large force of Germans resting and refitting in that area. The German division was alerted, and they attacked and killed or captured the whole American task force along with the escaping POWs, and we could not find out what happened to Billy before we left Europe. The wonderful news was that Billy had been captured, was alive, and was now on the way home.

On this operation General Patton's Third Army got some bad publicity. The rumor was that General Patton's son-in-law was in that POW Camp. Patton wanted his son-in-law out before the Germans found out who he was. The Germans would not have been nice to one of Patton's relatives. The newspapers in the States really made a big complaint about this daring operation. None of the newspapers mentioned how many hundreds of other POWs were in that camp.

■ ■ ■

Pacific Prospects

W e liked San Antonio. We liked the things that were done for us there, but home, Baton Rouge, was calling. Marie and I climbed aboard a train heading east, and as much as we wanted to see our friends in Houston, we didn't slow down. Our train connections were good, and we rolled into the station. There was a nice reception party waiting for us—Mother, Dad, Ida Marie (my sister), Mr. and Mrs. Roques, and Marie's sister and brother-in-law. We got a great welcome from them all, but I know Mother was the one who was happiest to see her youngest son all in one piece. I hoped this homecoming helped me to be forgiven for the many letters I could have written but didn't. Ned, Ida Marie's husband, could not come to the station; his brother "Jelly," an old friend of mine, had been killed on a bomber raid. It would have been too much for him to see me at that time.

The red carpet was rolled out for us; we were wined and dined, lent automobiles and fishing camps, and we were shuttled from one home to the other. Everyone was still under wartime rationing and many things were hard to get. Our families nonetheless made us welcome, sharing everything they had.

It was perfect relaxation, nearly. When I arrived in San Antonio, I had those orders in my pocket to return to the 8th Infantry Division after delivering General Weaver to Brooke General Hospital.

Before the General let Perko, Garman, and myself leave San Antonio, he called us into his hospital room and said, "We have been a good team, and I have enjoyed having you with me. Now, I am going to get well, and I want to go to the Pacific. I don't want to fight any more, but I want that campaign ribbon. Now, if you want to stay with me, that will be fine."

Thinking about those ten days I was using up, I was glad to tell the General: "I will be happy to go to the Pacific with you."

I wasn't a bit interested in going back to Europe. I had been offered a job as assistant to the G-3 (Plans and Operations) with the 8th Division, which meant I wouldn't have been wandering around in Repl' Depo's when I returned. Perko and Garman had the ten-day order just like I did, but I didn't know where they would end up if we went back to Europe, except that we would probably be split up. We had been together so long and had gone through so much with the General that we felt staying with him, staying together, was what we needed to do to finish our service.

General Weaver cancelled Perko's, Garman's, and my orders to go back to Europe, which suited all three of us. Marie and I went home. We began to introduce ourselves to each other again. Marie didn't quite understand what was the matter with me during the heavy thunder and lightning storms we had at night. I lay sweating, wanting to get under the bed. Days wore on, and some of this subsided. Sharp quick noises took longer to get used to—the little new noises at night, shades bumping the windows. There had been periods in the lines in the darkness when one's ears strained to detect any crawling, sliding, coughing, or mumbling. In the darkness in Baton Rouge, I was still doing the same.

I was surprised one day to run into Blue Flight leader Quentin Aanenson, the pilot who had knocked out the Tiger tank in Bergstein. When he had left for home, I was on my way back to the front, and neither of us thought we would see each other again, but we met in Stroube Drug Store. It turned out he had married a girl who lived on East Boulevard. He was rested and all of the strain had gone from his face. "Quint, is that you?" I asked. "You look so young—you looked like an old guy when I saw you last in Europe."

He replied, "Van, I thought *you* were old with the wrinkles you were carrying that day. When I saw you heading for the front when I left, I didn't think you would ever get home."

Soon we had to return to San Antonio. Billy Weaver had come home and had brought a fiancée with him. I think there must have been a whole lot of telephone conversation with Mrs. Weaver and General Weaver. Billy was scheduled to enter West Point—no problem with his combat experience, tank school and paratroop school behind him, to say nothing of the fact he would be a second generation Weaver at West Point. With the General's record in World War I and World War II, Billy wouldn't be hurting for support at all.

But there was a strict rule that you could not enter West Point as a plebe (freshman) if you were married. Billy chose the marriage.

The General and Mrs. Weaver wanted Marie and me to be in the wedding. It was summertime, so I was forced out of my winter wools and khakis into a suntan uniform. Marie thought it was fine looking. The gabardine was tailored for the wedding so it looked good even to me. The wedding was beautiful and everything seemed to go well for six weeks. Then Billy's wife's old prospect—old boyfriend—came back from the war, and there was a quick annulment, and Billy was left wondering how he got "took" so bad. No West Point. He went back on active duty as soon as he used up his overseas leave.

Perko and Garman were spending time at home, and I didn't expect to see them until the General called us together to go to the Pacific.

Marie and I were in San Antonio on May 8th when the news of V-E Day was shouted from the radios. All us soldiers were very happy. The idea that we were that much closer to being free to stay home, to do what we wanted to do, was great. How did I celebrate? I had been celebrating since I stepped off the *Ile de France*. The closer I got to Baton Rouge, the greater my feelings of elation grew.

Marie and I loved San Antonio, and we were still there when the Army boys began to come back from the War. We had a great time playing with the crowd. We went all over the city eating in

Mexican greasy spoons. I guess the ladies wondered what made us veterans drink so much, smoke so many packs of cigarettes. Well, I don't think we knew what was going on with us, either. I think that half of this wild group should have gone into the hospital and been checked over.

I first got my eye-opening, hair-raising, slow-down signal when Marie announced to me, "We are going to have a baby." That information was a great pleasure, but we had been having so much fun—everything was so carefree, the Army was taking care of us without our doing anything but living it up. Marie went to the baby doctor at Brooke General and he gave her information on diet, the amount of weight she could gain. This was all interesting, but I was having problems with this new potential responsibility. I didn't know very much about being a husband and now I was forced into thinking about being a father. I hadn't finished college, I had no prospects except to go to the Pacific—what would I do if I stayed home?

The only other prospect I had was what General Weaver offered when he heard the news: "If you stay in the service, I'll get you to Fort Benning as a river-crossing expert. You made two river crossings under combat conditions and you know what is necessary and how to line it up for successful operation. The Moselle crossing and the Roer Crossing, you were in on them from the planning stage to the end." I thought this over for a couple of days, and finally told the General that it was time Marie and I went home.

General didn't like this too much. But he told me that he had decided to retire as a Major General. If he waited too long he might have to go back to his permanent rank of Colonel. Retirement salary for a Major General is considerably better than a Colonel's.

Well, I made the decision to get out of the Army and come home. I was so proud of all the points that I had that would allow me to retire from active duty and join the Reserve Corps. Perko and Garman had enough points to stay home, too. We had a hard time leaving the General behind. He was father and friend to all of us. We had a sad good-bye supper at the Officer's Club, and then it was time to leave.

It really wasn't easy to leave active duty. I had grown up in the service. I had lived and breathed military service for nearly five years. Now I was wondering, "What in the world will I do?" I didn't know how I could go back to college and support a wife and baby to come. I had ruled out the railroad where my father worked. I loved the railroad—but to work for them? No. I went to Standard Oil of New Jersey, and they seemed to be glad I came.

Being employed by a big oil company seemed to be fine security for my wife and baby. I wanted to fit into civilian life so bad that it took some time to recognize that civilian workers' salaries were very low. I started working for the oil company at $152.00 per month. I had left a nice salary in the Army of $425.00 a month. I was certainly not achieving great things by coming home.

Nearly five years of working, learning, teaching military concepts, and serving in an all-out war for my country had made me a much better person. However, what I had learned did not serve me too well when I hung up my beloved uniform. My personal civilian war had just started.

Maj.
hurch

Brig-General
Weaver

Lt. Col.
Harris
Legion-of-
Merit

Lt. M.P.
Soldier's
medal

Brig-Ge
Russ